W9-ADD-586

LONELINESS

LONELINESS

CLARK E. MOUSTAKAS

A
Spectrum

Book

PRENTICE-HALL, INC.

152.4
Mo L

© 1961 BY
CLARK E. MOUSTAKAS

All rights reserved. No part of this book may be reproduced in any form, by mimeograph or any other means, without permission in writing from the publishers.

Library of Congress
Catalog Card No.: 61-13531

CLARK E. MOUSTAKAS is currently on the staff of the Merrill-Palmer Institute in Detroit, Michigan.

Current printing (last digit):

23 22 21 20 19 18 17

Printed in the United States of America
54016-C

Get ready to weep tears of sorrow
as bright as the brightest beads,
and like the bright beads you string
to wear round your throat at the burial,
gather your tears and string them
on a thread of your memory to wear around
your heart or its shattered fragments
will never come whole again.

From *Flamingo Feather* by Laurens van der Post,
reprinted with permission of The Hogarth Press
Ltd. and William Morrow & Co., Inc. 1949.

For Eve Winn

who lives within me
in the infinite loneliness
of the unique

PREFACE

The basic message in this book is that loneliness is a condition of human life, an experience of being human which enables the individual to sustain, extend, and deepen his humanity. Man is ultimately and forever lonely whether his loneliness is the exquisite pain of the individual living in isolation or illness, the sense of absence caused by a loved one's death, or the piercing joy experienced in triumphant creation. I believe it is necessary for every person to recognize his loneliness, to become intensely aware that, ultimately, in every fibre of his being, man is alone—terribly, utterly alone. Efforts to overcome or escape the existential experience of loneliness can result only in self-alienation. When man is removed from a fundamental truth of life, when he successfully evades and denies the terrible loneliness of individual existence, he shuts himself off from one significant avenue of his own self-growth.

I first began to discover the roots of my own loneliness during a family crisis when neither man nor reason could assuage the searing pain in my heart. This crisis was the instrument through which I plunged deeply into an intensive and timeless experience of the self. The sudden recognition and depth of my own loneliness was a revelation which changed the nature of my life. I could never again see the evening sun fading into oblivion without feeling lonely. I could never again pass a troubled person or see pain, misery, suffering, poverty around me without being deeply and sharply touched. This recognition of my own basic loneliness, this penetrating awareness of my own isolated existence, opened within me a flood of painful feeling and left me in a barren and eroded state. At the same time I saw life and nature in more vibrant forms than I had ever experienced before. Each aspect of my life took on a color, a distinctness and vividness, entirely new for me. Something extremely powerful took root in me and I came to know myself in a more honest and fuller sense than I ever thought possible. I learned that I could thrive in lonely silence. This recognition and meaningful awareness of myself as an utterly lonely person opened the way to deeper human bonds and associations and to a fuller valuing of all aspects of life and nature. I realized that man's inevitable and infinite loneliness is not solely an awful condition of human existence but that it is also the instrument through which man experiences new compassion and new beauty. It is this terror in loneliness which evokes new senses and makes possible the experiencing of deep companionship and radiant beauty.

My awareness of loneliness did not come as an idea but from the involvement of my whole being in loneliness. What I have written in this book is an experience of my own existence as a solitary individual, as well as the existence of others, and of the meaning which loneliness has for human growth. One can come to a recognition of loneliness as a condition of human life only through a deep and penetrating voyage of one's own solitary nature. I hope the experiences presented in the book will provide a primary source, an impetus to self-discovery, and to feeling-knowledge. I know that no person can remain unchanged once he opens himself to loneliness and surrenders himself to the terror and beauty of a totally isolated existence.

It is a great gift to be suddenly awakened, to perceive the world from vast, expansive inner openings and new pathways, to see light where there had been darkness, to find beauty in broken bits of stone, to see color where all had been dingy and gray, to hear a human voice and absorb a smile as a precious treasure, to see into the heart of life and to recognize the brevity of life and the necessity of making each moment count, to realize the ecstasy of human companionship—and when someone else sees this vital strand of lonely being not as an insight but with all the feeling of an informed heart, then how sweet is the confirmation. When someone cares enough to see into the deepest roots of one's nature, though it is heart-rending to be known in this naked sense, it brings the deepest measure of unique and thrilling sensations.

Loneliness for me started with a family crisis but my voyage took me into literature and music and art, into history and science. For many, many months I opened myself to the loneliness which surrounded me in my everyday living, to the lonely experiences of my colleagues, friends, and neighbors, to books and articles. I have concluded that loneliness is within life itself, and that all creations in some way spring from solitude, meditation, and isolation.

This work is not an exhaustive or comprehensive study, but is a pointed selection of lonely experiences and lonely persons, along with commentary on some of the conditions which penetrate human life and precipitate man's aloneness.

This book grows out of my own search to come to an understanding, awareness, and respect for myself as a solitary, isolated, lonely individual and the gripping, painful, exhilerating, and beautiful experience of being utterly alone and separated from others. In a sense, the book is an inquiry or search, perhaps a personal disclosure into the meaning and essence of loneliness itself, the loneliness of my life and the loneliness of others, which has shaken and stirred me profoundly and opened new channels of awareness and beauty in the world.

Man has recognized the importance of companionship. Perhaps this book can strike a chord into the lonely life of others, can be one step not only in experiencing the real terror in loneliness but also in revealing new horizons of love and beauty.

Acknowledgments

I wish to thank the many persons who conversed with me and wrote to me so openly and intimately of their experiences with loneliness, particularly Florence Bedell, Paul Jensen, James Byars, and Glen Christensen. I also thank Melvyn Baer who created an atmosphere in which much of the writing was done, Dorothy Lee for her many suggestions in helping me to be myself in this book, Pauline Knapp and the Merrill-Palmer Institute for enabling me to work in my own way, Miss Esther Betz of the University of Michigan Law Library who entrusted to me for an indefinite period the ten volumes of the transcript and documents of the second Hiss trial, Connie Jones who helped prepare the manuscript for publication, Betty Moustakas who stood by silently sharing my pain and suffering during many of my encounters with loneliness, and Jim and Thelma Dimas, Minnie Berson, Eugene Alexander and David Smillie, each in his own way bringing me new depths of feeling and awareness to bear the solitude and isolation and to grow in it. I thank Grace Darling for her inspiring guidance and encouragement during the long wait when she envisioned "Loneliness" as a full-length story rather than as a professional article.

Particularly and especially, I wish to express my gratitude to my daughter, Kerry, without whom this book would not have been started and without whom my own self-discovery would have been delayed or permanently denied.

TABLE OF CONTENTS

LONELINESS

I

THE TERROR AND LOVE IN LONELINESS

I have experienced loneliness many times in my life but until recently I lived my loneliness without being aware of it. In the past I tried to overcome my sense of isolation by plunging into work projects and entering into social activities. By keeping busy and by committing myself to interesting and challenging work, I never had to face, in any direct or open way, the nature of my own existence as an isolated and solitary individual.

I first began to awaken to the meaning of loneliness, to feel loneliness in the center of my consciousness, one terrible day when my wife and I were confronted with the necessity of making a decision. We were told that our five-year-old daughter, Kerry, who had a congenital heart defect, must have immediate surgery. We were warned, gently but firmly, by the cardiologist that failure to operate would cause continual heart deterioration and premature death. At the same time he informed us that there were many unknown factors in heart surgery and that with Kerry's particular defect there was about twenty per cent chance that she would not survive the operation.

What were we to do? We experienced a state of acute worry, followed by a paralyzing indecision that lasted several days.

There was no peace or rest for me, anywhere, at this time. I, who had known Kerry as a vigorous, active child, bursting with energy, whether on roller skates, a two-wheel bike, or in the pool, was suddenly forced to view her as handicapped. In spite of her exuberance and her seemingly inexhuastible energy, there in my mind was the report of the X-rays and the catharization showing a significant perforation and enlargement of her heart.

1

Visions of my daughter were constantly before me. I roamed the streets at night searching for some means, some resource in the universe which would guide me to take the right step. It was during these desperate days and nights that I first began to think seriously of the inevitable loneliness of life. I was overcome with the pain of having to make a decision, as a parent, which had potentially devastating consequences either way. If I decided on surgery, she might not survive the operation. If I decided against it, the possibility of a premature death would always haunt me. It was a terrible responsibility, being required to make a decision, a life or death decision, for someone else. This awful feeling, this overwhelming sense of responsibility, I could not share with anyone. I felt utterly alone, entirely lost, and frightened; my existence was absorbed in this crisis. No one fully understood my terror or how this terror gave impetus to deep feelings of loneliness and isolation which had lain dormant within me. There at the center of my being, loneliness aroused me to a self-awareness I had never known before.

At last a decision was made, primarily by my wife, that we had no choice but to go ahead with the surgery, immediately, while we were both alive and able to give Kerry our strength and love. We explained the problem to Kerry simply. She quickly accepted the idea of the operation with that measureless trust and confidence which, a young child feels with parents long before there is any understanding of trust or confidence.

The time of waiting during the operation itself was filled with painful anguish, terrifying suspension, and restlessness—but the most terrible loneliness of all occurred several days later.

I stood in the dark hallway of the hospital, a place I had repeatedly traversed with restless and weary footsteps. Kerry lay beside me in her wheelcart watching television. The light reflected in her eyes as she watched the program. Momentarily the shots, the tubes, the large incision across her chest were forgotten. I do not know how long I stood beside her. My mind was empty of all thought and feeling. Suddenly she looked at me. There were tears in her eyes. "Daddy, why is that little boy crying?" she asked. I looked for a moment, then I knew; I saw an episode I had witnessed many times in the past week.

The boy's eyes were transfixed, glued to the windows, looking below— expectant, watchful, waiting. Waiting for someone to come to protect and comfort him. Waiting for someone to rescue him from abandonment. Waiting. There was no one. He was alone—totally, utterly alone. Outside, people moved rapidly up and down steps and along the walk. Cars hurried down the highway. Inside, the public address blared out doctors' names. Nurses' aides shouted to children to get to sleep. But this child sat up in bed—his small body rigid—his heart breaking. Waiting. I knew in that moment he experienced a crushing loneliness, a feeling of being deserted and forsaken. He was quiet and frightened. Silent tears slipped down his face. What could I say to Kerry? She wept in sympathy. She did not expect an answer.

When I could no longer bear his suffering I entered the room. I stood quietly beside him for several minutes. Then the words came, "I know. Right now there's no one. No one at all. Your Mama has left you." He burst into painful, racking sobs and sighs. His grief was momentarily broken. All his silent agony burst into convulsive moans and piercing cries. A nurse entered. She glared at me. She spoke angrily, "Now see what you've done. Why don't you leave him alone?" Then, turning to him, she spoke firmly, "You know your mother isn't here. She left you after supper. She told you she'd be back in the morning. All the crying and shouting you can do will not bring her back. Stop. Stop now. You're keeping the other children awake. Lie down. Go to sleep. Your mother will come tomorrow." I stood by silently; as the nurse left the room, I followed her.

Walking beside her, I said, "You can't leave him that way. He is painfully lonely. He feels cut-off from all meaningful ties. He will harbor this terror a long time. Go back. Tell him you care. Hold his hand. Say something gentle." She answered, "I can't. I have other duties." I suggested, "Tell him you would like to stay but you have certain duties to finish first—that you will look in again soon." Hesitating a few moments, the nurse returned to the child's room. She spoke softly this time, "I'm sorry your mother isn't here with you now when you want her. I must give out medicine to other children but I'll be back. Maybe this will help," and she handed him a sucker.

Beside Kerry again, I could see a faint smile cross the child's face as he put the sucker in his mouth. There was a moment of peace. Then the silent tears continued to flow until he slipped into heavy, uncomfortable sleep with the sucker still in his mouth. I knew he would never forget this experience of loneliness just as I would never forget sitting alone in my daughter's room waiting for the slow, restorative process following her heart surgery.

For many hours I had been forced to ration to Kerry small cubes of ice—just enough to moisten her lips and mouth—one small piece each half hour. In between Kerry's begging, pleading voice asked for more. I had stated the limit directly and told her why it was necessary. But her lips were dry. She had been without liquids almost forty-eight hours. I felt dry too. I wanted to share this experience with her and had refrained from liquids myself. I felt her extreme thirst and yet worked feverishly to arouse her interest in other matters. Each new thought excited her momentarily but she always returned to the cry for ice, entreating with such urgency that each episode left me feeling the oppressor. The hours passed slowly and finally the glorious moment arrived when a real portion of liquids could be taken. The surgeon ordered a full glass of Coke. She drank it in a frenzy in two or three gulps and within a few minutes fell into a heavy sleep. I was exhausted, feeling her anguish, hearing her distressing cries for ice, exhausted with the effort of distraction and diversion.

It was a peaceful time. I was alone. I felt elated, full—yet empty, and a strange aura of peacefulness settled within me. I stared blankly at the floor. I do not know what forces within me caused me to glance at Kerry, but as I did in an instant an absolute terror overcame me. Suddenly I felt completely desolate and alone. I was aware of being depressed by and conscious of my own solitude. Something vague, hidden, crucial was before me. I could not understand but something seemed wrong in the way she was sleeping.

I noticed a slight tensing, her arms pulled away from her body, the fingers twisted and extended. Her entire body grew rigid. She went into a series of jerky, stretching movements—contortions—convulsions—grotesque and terrifying. Immediately I realized she was having a brain seizure. Her entire being was in a state of extreme agitation. She began biting her tongue. I slipped a pencil in her mouth, shouted for the nurse, and urged that the surgeon be called immediately. The nurse looked in briefly and left. I stroked Kerry's hair and whispered her name, but each time I touched her she moved away with violent, gross movements. I had to hold her body because she twisted and turned so violently there was danger she would fall off the bed. In those moments I experienced indescribable loneliness and fear and shock. In some measure my body writhed with Kerry's. I paced, and stretched, and turned as I witnessed the seizure. The most intolerable feeling was the realization that she was beyond my reach, beyond my voice and touch. She was in pitiful plight—entirely by herself. She was without anyone or anything. I tried to commune with her. I whispered her name softly, gently, over and over again. "Kerry, Kerry. Kerry, my darling. It's Daddy. I'm here right beside you. I won't leave. Kerry, I'm here. Kerry. Kerry. Kerry." She opened her eyes. A horrible sound issued from her throat—then several more utterances of anguish and pain and fear. She screamed three words as she saw me—three awful words filled with agony and stark terror—words and tones that I shall never forget—*"No You Bad."* I answered, "It's all right, Kerry. It's Daddy. I'm here. I'm beside you." Her entire body was stiff, yet in constant motion. She jerked up and down, flailed her arms and legs at me, and tried to kick me. I was certain she did not recognize me. She was in a state of shock and experiencing a semi-conscious nightmare. In her dim state of awareness she thought I was a doctor who was about to administer a shot. The muscles in her face were tight. The mouth was open and the jaws distended and distorted. The stretching and agitated movement continued as she seemed to be struggling to escape, to find comfort, to find a resting place.

At last the surgeon arrived, took one look and shouted to the nurse, "Brain Edema. I'll have to give her a shot of glucose." The word "shot" struck the center of her terror. She tried to form words to speak, but no sound came; she shook violently in an effort to scream out an alarm. Then came an instinctual cry, emitted from deep within her being, a cry of raving terror followed by excruciating moans. I continued saying her name, whispering softly, gently, trying to offer strength, knowing all the while that she was lost to me yet knowing also that I alone realized her pain and terror. Her wails were so piercingly effective they reverberated ceaselessly everywhere inside me and in the room. The doctor asked me to leave but I refused; I knew I had to stay whatever happened. Kerry's eyes were wide and fitful. She continued moaning and uttering the weird, painful cries. The nurse pushed me aside to hold Kerry while the shot was being administered. Only a small amount had been injected when Kerry gave such a violent jerk that the nurse let go and the needle fell out. Again the moaning continued and one word rang out distinctly, clearly—a plea, a beseeching, final cry for help. She held the word "Mama" a long, long time and then the moans and furious motions and cries resumed. I held her arms as the surgeon inserted the needle again. She looked at me with utter contempt and hatred. Her eyes were full of pain and accusation. I whispered, "I know how much it hurts." I could feel her pain and terror in my own nerves and bones and tissues and blood, but at the same time I knew in that moment no matter how fervently I lived through it with her, how much I wanted to share it with her, I knew, she was alone, beyond my reach. I wanted so much for her to feel my presence, but she could not. She was beyond my call, beyond the call of anyone. It was her situation in a world entirely and solely her own. There was nothing further I could do. Each time she screamed her voice ripped through me, penetrating deeply into my inner being.

At last it was finished. The nurse put up the sides of the bed. Then she and the surgeon left. It was dark. Kerry and I were alone again.

Kerry's cries and the grotesque, agitated body movements continued. All I could do was stand by. I tried to stroke her forehead but when I touched her she stiffened, screamed in pain, and moved violently away. I wanted her to know I was there, extending my compassion; I wanted her to see I suffered too; I wanted her to realize I had not left her. So I repeated over and over again, "My darling, Kerry. My sweet, Kerry. I'm here. Right here. Daddy is beside you. I won't leave you. Not ever. Not ever."

At length, she fell asleep. I left her room and stood outside her door to keep anyone from entering to disturb her. I stood in a frozen position for several hours, not moving at all, completely without feeling, and in a state of total nothingness. I tried in many ways to express this experience immediately afterwards but I could not. It remained within me, a tremendous constricted mass. Each time I tried to form a word the mass rose within me and I choked and sputtered and the muscles in my body tightened. My mouth closed. The sounds were shut off and the intense experience settled inside me again. There was no way to share this loneliness, this experience of fear, and shock, and isolation. It was an experience which held its own integrity but was so far-reaching and sharp, so utterly pervasive and gripping, that when I tried to speak only weird and painful cries, like Kerry's, came from me. I distinctly felt that I had failed her and that she had faced this great crisis alone.

Later she remembered the doctor who held her while a shot was given her but she did not remember her father who stayed beside her during the terrible ordeal and who suffered along with her, totally isolated and alone. As I dwell upon this experience of mutual loneliness, I realize how completely beyond my most imaginative comprehension is the heart surgery itself, when my daughter lay on the operating table and her heart was removed from her body while a mechanical pump pushed blood through her arteries and veins. Is the horror of this lonely existence perceivable or knowable at all? What does it mean in the life and growth of an individual child?

Kerry remained in the hospital two weeks. When we took her home, she was completely recovered physically but her nightmares and terrors continued for several months after she left the hospital.

During the two weeks while she was in the pediatric ward, we never left her side. I had many opportunities to observe children experiencing isolation and loneliness. It was at this time that I felt a strong urge to look into the heart of the lonely experience. Starting with these experiences before and during the hospitalization, I began to discover the meaning of loneliness. I began to see that loneliness is neither good nor bad, but a point of intense and timeless awareness of the Self, a beginning which initiates totally new sensitivities and awarenesses, and which results in bringing a person deeply in touch with his own existence and in touch with others in a fundamental sense. I began to see that in the deepest experiences the human being can know—the birth of a baby, the prolonged illness or death of a loved relative, the loss of a job, the creation of a poem, a painting, a symphony, the grief of a fire, a flood, an accident—each in its own way touches upon the roots of loneliness. In each of these experiences, in the end, we must go alone.

In such experiences, inevitably one is cut off from human companionship. But experiencing a solitary state gives the individual the opportunity to draw upon untouched capacities and resources and to realize himself in an entirely unique manner. It can be a new experience. It may be an experience of exquisite pain, deep fear and terror, an utterly terrible experience, yet it brings into awareness new dimensions of self, new beauty, new power for human compassion, and a reverence for the precious nature of each breathing moment.

II

THE EXPERIENCE OF BEING LONELY

There is a power in loneliness, a purity, self-immersion, and depth which is unlike any other experience. Being lonely is such a total, direct, vivid existence, so deeply felt, so startlingly different, that there is no room for any other perception, feeling, or awareness. Loneliness is an organic experience which points to nothing else, is for no other purpose and results in nothing but the realization of itself. Loneliness is not homelessness. There is no departure or exile, the person is fully there, as fully as he ever can be.

Loneliness involves a unique substance of self, a dimension of human life which taps the full resources of the individual. It calls for strength, endurance, and sustenance, enabling a person to reach previously unknown depths and to realize a certain nakedness of inner life.

Being lonely is a reality of far-reaching social consequence, yet it is distinctly a private matter. It is an experience of raw sensitivity. It is so entirely pure and complete that there is no room for anything else or anyone else. Feelings of loneliness take root deeply and unfold in varied directions. Being lonely involves a certain pathway, requires a total submersion of self, a letting be of all that is and belongs, a staying or remaining with the situation, until a natural realization or completion is reached; when a lonely existence completes itself, the individual becomes, grows from it, reaches out for others in a deeper, more vital sense.

8

1.*

Elizabeth was and never ceases to be. Her whole life consisted of being. We, who knew her intimately became infinitely richer in love and understanding because of her being. She gave with no thought of giving, she loved with no thought of being loved, and she received and created love because she was lovable.

We, her parents, her sister of nine, and her brother of six, had waited for her arrival with joy. We prepared for her with loving thoughts and plans, with shopping and sewing and sharing. She began to be and we were happy.

We wanted her to be born at home and the doctor consented. The night of her arrival came and she was born attended by the family doctor, her grandmother, her loving aunt, her father, and, of course, me, her mother. The joyful cry of a newborn baby filled the room and then I heard that moment of such quiet silence. Something strange was happening and I was filled with the fear of impending disaster. A baby girl was born, but the doctor, there in that room which was suddenly filled with the anxiety of vitally concerned persons, had to say to all of us that Elizabeth, our baby, through some unforeseen, unpredictable, unknown reason, had failed to develop properly. One of the lower vertebrae had not grown together. This allowed the spinal fluid to escape and form a cyst near the end of her spinal column. Her body was paralyzed below this vertebra, and one foot, especially, had not developed in a normal fashion. However, Elizabeth *was*, and, being herself as she was at that moment, she created a deep feeling of reverence for life which bound us all together in that moment of shock and despair which none of us shall forget. The lesion was so severe that the doctor felt that Elizabeth should be in a hospital. He was a brave man, with a strength and depth of feeling which I had never suspected, as he had often seemed rather brusk and hurried and unfeeling. But this night he could tell us that we could not expect our baby to live but a very few days, that her condition was so serious it could not be treated by medicine or by operation. Perhaps because he had the courage to be honest and because he expected us to have the strength to face our suffering, we were able to do this, at least partially.

---

* The illustrations in this chapter are taken from actual situations, either directly from my own experience or from the experience of others, conveyed to me in written or spoken form.

Her grandmother and her Aunt Emma bathed and dressed Elizabeth. She was a beautiful baby with soft brown hair and a little round face. Margaret and Paul were gently awakened and came in so happily to see the new baby. But so soon we had to tell them that she was not well and must go to the hospital where they had better facilities for taking care of her. They each held her for a few moments and kissed her goodbye. I felt that my very heart would break.

For three days I was numb with grief and shock, with disbelief and pain. I thought I would turn my face to the wall until it was all over and maybe I would never need to look straight into the face of my grief and disappointment. We wanted her, loved her, and longed to keep her. Then that feeling of shame and mortification crept in. We, Clarence and I, had a child that was deformed, was not normal, could we face our relatives and our friends now? What had we done to deserve this kind of punishment? If we had done wrong why should Elizabeth be the one to pay for it? I searched my soul for the meaning of life and for the meaning of Elizabeth's being.

Three days went by, the allotted time the doctor had given her to live, and Elizabeth *was*. The nurses and specialists at the hospital wondered at her fragile yet tenacious hold on life. A week passed by, and two weeks. Elizabeth *was* and would not be denied. The doctor said we could have her at home. He felt that we could care for her if they taught me how to keep the cyst covered with Vaseline and gauze. But he said we could not expect her to live even from one day to the next. Her death might occur rather suddenly at any time.

I had had two weeks to wrestle with myself. I had had many well-wishing visitors who either talked too much, or were tongue-tied through embarrassment and indecision. I experienced many new thoughts and new feelings during these days. I found the meaning of living one moment at a time. I could only live one moment at a time for I didn't have the strength to endure more than one moment. I found I could not plan before time what I would say to this person or that person. I could only say what was to be said at the moment when it arrived. I found myself raw with sensitivity to the feelings and embarrassments of my guests and I found a deeper, softer bond between the four of us at home, waiting for Elizabeth to join us. But perhaps more than all of these I found that the length of the life span or the conditions of a person's body do not detract from the meaning and value of being. I could accept Elizabeth without apology to anyone.

We went together to bring her home. This was a moment of joy and sadness. We were together but there were many things we were unable to do for Elizabeth because of her fragile condition. We could not hold her or cuddle her because it was painful for her to be moved. She could be comfortable only on either one side or the other on a firm pillow. We could be close to her, hold her hand, and sing to her, but we couldn't cuddle and comfort her when she cried.

At this time I had another difficult decision to make. I was tempted to bathe and dress the baby before the children awakened in the morning. But bathing the baby was one thing Margaret and Paul had been anticipating for a long time. Now, Elizabeth was a perfectly beautiful, normal baby above the defective vertebra, and guests would remark about what a pretty healthy baby she was, unless they were aware of her difficulty. So should I try to bathe her and dress her alone to protect the other children from the pain of realizing Elizabeth's real physical condition? They were so eager to be with the baby and to help with everything that I decided I must be honest and we must all live through this experience together. The impact of this experience for me is inexpressible. The children were so happy to do something for Elizabeth. They thought her little foot was so delicate and beautiful. Bath time became a meaningful experience every day in which we each had a part. For a while Elizabeth cried when we gave her a bath and I was afraid it was a painful, physical ordeal for her. But I found her looking at my face and saw that I had an anxious tense expression. I started to smile and we sometimes sang softly or hummed a little during the bath and Elizabeth responded by being happy and not crying.

She lived day after day and because we knew we could not expect to keep her we found joy in each moment that we did have her. In this way I found that this was the way that I wanted to live all of the time—each moment to the extent of its possibilities. I learned that, although I could make plans and anticipate the future, life is demanding and unpredictable. In order to live I must be sensitive to these demands and be flexible enough to experience them. We, as a family, found joy and an increase of love, acceptance and understanding.

Five months went by and Elizabeth, even through the reality of her pain and immobility, remained loving, giving, and beautiful by being herself. She looked at me with her big brown eyes, which seemed like deep pools of liquid pain, and she talked with me with wisdom and understanding almost beyond my comprehension.

The doctors and nurses and other people wondered and were amazed that she continued to live. Elizabeth, by being, seemed to release the love of all the persons who knew her and this releasing of love seemed to spread throughout her family, which included grandparents, aunts, uncles, and cousins. Love spread to the neighbors, to friends, to persons in other communities and other states. People who met her were not moved by pity but seemed to become filled with a gentleness and sensitivity. It seemed that Elizabeth was suspended in a rich atmosphere of love which sustained her and permitted us to keep her with us beyond even our expectations.

Then the night came; Clarence and I had always taken turns watching her through the long nights, but this night we watched together as her breathing became slower and slower until it seemed she would not breathe again. We held her hands because she seemed to feel comforted by this and because we wanted to hold her hands. The night wore on and at almost dawn for some strange reason Clarence and I both went to sleep for a very few minutes, and then awakened very quickly with a sharpness and clarity of mind and soul. Elizabeth was still and the eastern sky was filled with light as the sun burst forth in the glory of the sunrise. And Margaret and Paul with their playmates picked yellow roses and gave them to Elizabeth.

2.

No one understood. No one cared enough to let him live his life his way, and he was not strong enough, not courageous enough, to stand alone. Suffering with tuberculosis, he wanted a program of home treatment, but he was unsuccessful in finding a physician who would care for him. He could not find anyone with whom to share his shattering illness. In the end, his wife and father withdrew their support and told him he had no choice but to enter an institution. The final blow came in the form of a court order instigated by the city health department to force him into a hospital.

Bill Downs was completely alone then. He felt his life slipping away. He tried to tell his family he was losing control. Unable to think clearly or talk decisively, he spoke in a confused and desultory manner, in dejected tones. He felt isolated and doomed and on the verge of being destroyed. His inner life was gone. There was nothing left for him but a meaningless existence. He tried in every way to find a way but he felt utterly rejected. He knew with dreaded clarity he would be compelled to enter a sanitarium where there could only be loneliness without relief, days without sunshine and trees and fresh air, nights without the wind and stars and moon, and a life without freedom and joy and love.

After many sleepless nights, one gloomy dawn, he arose and without a word, left the house, driving his car to the hospital. He was inducted in a mechanical way, and placed in a small room with four other men. He was told that hospital rules were precise, that he would be put on a strict regime, and would be expected to remain in bed at all times as immobile as possible. Bill noticed his roommates for the first time. He learned that they all spoke only in a foreign language. He would not be able to talk with them. They lay there silent, listless, and severely emaciated. As Bill watched them, the numbness suddenly disappeared. He was seized with a feeling of helpless fear, a feeling so strong that it twisted and turned everywhere in his body. He felt completely removed from the world, utterly alone. He lay back on the pillow overcome with terrifying thoughts. Several hours passed; a tray of food was brought to him. It was tasteless and cold. Tears rolled down his face as he remembered the personal value and significance of his meals at home. His wife created meals with love to serve his heart as well as his appetite. The food before him was ugly, intended only to satiate hunger. He could not eat. He choked as he tried. Food mattered to him only within a shared experience. He felt empty, nauseated. Sharp fear hit him again. His mind whirled. He felt terrifying panic. He knew he would die if he stayed in the sanitarium. The urge to live welled strong in him again. There was only one way. He had to leave, to run, anywhere. He threw on his clothes and ran wildly out of the hospital.

The drive home was a nightmare. The anxiety was so strong he was totally unaware of what he was doing, where he was going. Tears streamed down his face. He struggled with choking sensations and feelings of agony. The whole world seemed against him but he would not quit. He would not die without a fight.

Somehow he reached his home and collapsed on the couch. When his wife saw him her mind blurred and dizzily she knelt beside him. She put her arms around him. In the torrent of misery, time passed and the intense painful feelings of loneliness and isolation subsided again to a state of numbness.

They were together again. This time in hopelessness. Their courage, faith, and conviction had disappeared long ago. But they were reunited. Hurriedly, Mrs. Downs packed their suitcases. She felt that time was precious. She had to hurry. She knew they would have to keep running. She had to stay alive, keep them going. She felt she had failed her husband once. Without knowing it, she had joined the forces against him. She knew she had to help in restoring his faith, not realizing she had lost her own, not knowing she could not strengthen him because she too was friendless, and weak, and alone.

Somehow they left the house to say goodbye to their son and Mr. Downs' father. As they saw these treasured faces, the disintegrating anxiety and loneliness overcame them again. This time they collapsed in separate parts of the house. Frightening feelings shook them completely, subsided momentarily and returned. There was no way to talk to them, to give them hope and renew their courage or to convey human sympathy in any way. The scene severely disturbed the elder Mr. Downs. Little Roger was deeply troubled too. He only partly understood the meaning of his parents' utter misery. At first father and son tried to talk to the parents, but Mr. and Mrs. Downs could no longer hear any human voice. They were experiencing the most crushing feeling of isolation and worthlessness they had ever known, an experience so complete no other perception was possible. In time grandfather and grandson felt the futility of their efforts and went to another part of the house to sit and wait in silent tears.

Then the telephone rang. It was Mrs. Gans from the health department. She brought the family back to fearful reality and the urgency of flight. She threatened the senior Mr. Downs, quietly and politely, "If you do not see that your son returns to the sanitarium by morning I will issue a warrant for the police department to pick him up and take him forcibly." Mr. Downs could not talk. He replaced the receiver, rested for a moment, then approached his children to tell them they must hurry.

Mr. and Mrs. Downs somehow mustered enough strength to get into their car and drive toward a distant spot. After driving a short while, the shocking truth that inner peace and unity were gone, that their family was broken, struck them so sharply with a flood of frightened feeling, they had to stop to rest and recover enough energy to go ahead.

A few days later a policeman called the senior Mr. Downs. He gave his first name and indicated he was a friend of Mr. Downs. He wanted to locate him. Mr. Downs asked, "What do you want him for?" The officer stated calmly, "We have a warrant for his arrest and I want to pick him up." Mr. Downs replied, "I have no idea where he is but I can assure you he is out of the state." The officer continued, "We have to be absolutely sure about it. I did not want to cause him any embarrassment or anything, but I thought maybe if I were the one who picked him up, it would be easier for him to come along."

Local policemen contacted friends and neighbors of the family to locate Mr. Downs. The story they told was always the same. They were looking for Bill Downs because he had a severe, contagious illness which could easily infect others. One policeman was especially violent in his objection to home treatments. He protested to the neighbors that he would not want a tubercular patient living next door to him. "Just think," he said, "every morning you'd wake up. The milkman would pick up his empty bottles and the next day he'd bring the filled bottles back to your house. You'd be drinking out of the same bottles that he used the day before, maybe infecting yourself and your children."

Gradually the neighbors in immediate proximity erected barriers to separate their property from the Downs', as though even the house and the land were afflicted. They told the senior Mr. Downs they would not want Bill or his family back in the neighborhood until his illness was completely arrested.

In time, the Downs' personal belongings and furniture were stored among many relatives in different parts of the state. Their home was sold. There was nothing left to remind neighbors or health and police officials that a diseased family had once lived within their boundaries and endangered community living. But at the same time, there was nothing left of meaning and value in the health department, or in neighborliness; for in the process of destroying the Downs family and forcing them into a lonely and estranged existence, communal humanity and the commandment of "Love thy neighbor" were broken too.

3.

What was most painful for me about my mother's dying of cancer in a city hospital was the feeling of not knowing if, in her dying moments and days, she knew I was there with her, trying to talk with her, comfort her, and love her. For two years she had fought the cancer, trying to become healthy again, making visits to the clinic—all the time becoming physically weaker, thinner, and more jaundiced. Slowly the cancer created a barrier between her and her family, between life and health, arousing feelings of anxiety, concern, and helplessness in all of us. She kept her pain and torment to herself, trying to be herself and make a life, trying to hold off impending death.

I arrived at the city hospital, where my mother lay dying, at one-thirty A.M., two days before the Fourth of July. I was taken to her ward room which was also occupied by five other women. The rest of our family, my older brother and sister, my brother-in-law, and a very close friend of the family, almost like a father, sat in the waiting room, despondent in the July heat, waiting anxiously for death to come. The doctors told us she had only hours to live and would not pull through the night.

I had not seen my mother since Christmas. Then her body was becoming very frail, but she had managed to appear strong and jovial in making a Christmas celebration for all of us. For she was that way, no matter what befell her—poverty, illness, or deep hurt—she would pull together all her resources and fight what had to be fought within herself, not wanting others to know the real agony she was facing.

I became panic-stricken as I approached my mother's bed, passing by the other women in the ward without a notice, not even stopping to talk to my family. I saw my mother's completely jaundiced face. Her neck and arms had become so thin her veins and bone-joints protruded. She was under sedation and breathing heavily. Her mouth was parched and the dry skin on her lips was cracked. My whole being became filled with shock and fright, and disgust at what had been done to my mother by the cancer.

I kissed my mother's forehead. In a quivering, crying voice, with tears streaming from my eyes, I spoke, "It's me, your son, Paul. I have finally arrived. I am here." There was no answer, no gesture of recognition. She did not lift her hands to my face; she did not embrace me as she had always done before. She lay there, breathing heavily, in agonized gasps. I felt the awful chasm between us; my voice was calling to her, talking to her, crying for her, but there was no answer, no response. I stroked her hair and forehead more than an hour, without stopping to rest or talk to anyone. Then our close friend was at the bedside with me, tears trickling out of his eyes, too, for the woman he had loved so genuinely. I could not talk to him at all. My throat was choked with tearful hurting and a terrible upsurging of lonely, helpless feeling. I refused to sink into loneliness. In her fight now I wanted to fight with her, to suffer for her, to be strong for her. That was all it was humanly possible for me to do, all I could do. Inside I tried to feel with her, to fight with her, for this I knew she was doing inside, even though she could not talk or respond to me.

She lived until the Sunday morning after the Fourth of July, occasionally during Friday and Saturday morning stirring and asking for some liquid on her lips or to have her position changed. This was the only kind of communication that came from her.

That Thursday night was the most difficult, but it was difficult all the way, for the feelings of warmth that kept trying to emerge and be expressed were futile and frustrated by my mother's inability to respond to me. I so much wanted to tell her that I had come to realize what a good mother she had really been to me, how much her relation to me had meant in my growth, despite all the arguments, the hurts, and the hates that I had felt so many times in my life. The doctors came in and out through the four days, checking her intravenous feeding apparatus, checking her heart beat, giving her needles. The nurses came in to see if she were all right, the aides came occasionally to bathe her. The other patients had visitors, talking jovially and happily about going home soon, while my family felt the agony of my mother's dying and waited for it to be over. We had a hard time to keep from feeling that she was already dead, taken from us. It was difficult not to become impersonal toward her, not to talk about the funeral arrangements.

Saturday morning my mother was put under an oxygen tent because her breathing had become such painful gasps for air, for life itself. She struggled so to respond to those around her. This day, the feelings of warmth—and those of separation and loneliness—were mingled with the suffering for and with her. I stood by her side as the doctors flicked their fingers before my mother's eyes, and checked her heart, and told me that she was not in contact, that all she was aware of or could feel or respond to was physical sensation, pains in her body or the prick of a needle going into her thin, frail arms.

Some of the family, and I too, talked about funeral arrangements when the doctors stated that she was not in contact and that she would die very shortly. I was bothered by this kind of talk, even though I knew it was important to get things worked out. I could not accept the fact of the impersonality of it and soon I began to feel angry with myself.

Then my mother's eyes opened a little. She looked around the oxygen tent, frightened and dazed by where she found herself. She seemed to be trying to fight her way out of the oxygen tent, out of the bed and the hospital, into life and health. I felt she was alive again and feared she heard us talking about the funeral arrangements. I told the family to talk outside, that Momma was awake. They stopped talking and looked on as I talked with my mother, telling her not to be afraid of the oxygen tent, that it was there to help her breathe. She groaned and tried to turn her head toward me. My whole family felt that she was in contact with life again and talked with her, although the only signs of awareness that she showed were her groans and the moving of her eyes. She had a tear on the side of her eye, as though it hurt to be dying and to hear her family talk of a funeral for her, but it seemed to be this hurt that enabled her to make contact again with us. I felt warmth surging within me and, finally overcoming my impersonal feelings, felt again that this was my mother, and that no matter if she were dying of cancer I had to care for her, be with her, and suffer with her until death did actually come; otherwise it would be all wrong, all foolish and awful. Above all I had to remain her son and maintain the deepest relationship with her until the final moment.

It was this that helped me work through some of my hurt and lonely feelings, and feel a little alive. This seeming wakefulness of my mother did not last very long, only a few hours, but it captured the whole family. It made us more compassionate in our caring for her, stroking her forehead, getting the doctors to give her needles when she was in pain, and putting liquids on her parched lips and tongue. I talked with her, telling her where she was, telling her not to fear about needing to take care of things. She seemed to hear me. I went on to tell her about my wife and her grandson. It made me feel again that I was her son and she was my mother. It made me feel again that though I might not be completely heard by her, at least it was important to be there, not to look at her impersonally as someone dying, as out of reach already by death. It made me feel that it was not futile to continue to care, that I must keep trying to feel for and with her, that I must live each moment with her.

She went back into a coma a few hours after she opened her eyes; the whole ward was filled with her agonizing gasping for breath. It seemed to be her last communication with the world, with her family, and with me. This was now her voice. It helped me to maintain the personal warmth and concern for her, which for a time I had almost given up, not realizing how important it was to be a person to her even in the face of death.

The funeral arrangements, the sitting in the funeral parlor, the burial, were all unreal. A rush of time overtook me; I felt weak and exhausted and guilty—a failure, because I had not come to see my mother earlier, to talk with her, to eat with her, to laugh with her. I felt deeply lonely because I felt that despite all my attempts I had failed to communicate with her, had failed to give her enough of myself, so that she could respond. I felt miserable because I had failed so many times in the past to respond to her help, to accept the warmth and love she tried to give me. Another wave of loneliness overcame me as I considered the times when I fought her, hated her, and pushed her away from me.

Then there was something beyond the guilt and isolation. There was the feeling that in the agony of it all, in the bitter moments of twisted emotions, loneliness and separation, I had received a sense of eternity through my mother. This time in her giving, I was free to accept and ready to feel and receive from her. She gave me many personal and important feelings and values, ultimates seeded in her dying moments Through her I came to see that in the desperate moments of actuality that seem to overtake us we overlook the fact that in each moment, in each of us, eternity itself is embedded.

What makes death significant is the awareness of the uniqueness of each relationship we have. This was my mother; the word "mother" brings on a flow of feeling and past experiences and years of living together, loving together, and hating, too. The fighting and conflicts do not seem important anymore, the arguments and intense pains and emotions that clouded the relationship have evaporated. This was my mother, and I realize the uniqueness of our relationship. It was not an impersonal fact of someone having cancer and dying, but it was a basic relationship that can never be repeated, a piece of eternity, never to be the same anywhere. These actual moments with her are mine forever. In her dying, I was able to become open to myself and to my mother, to claim our relationship, to look back upon the past in quick moments while at her bedside and realize the times she did give me warmth and love, and the times when pain and emotional conflict blocked the giving and the receiving.

Through my mother's dying and through my loneliness, I gained a sense of the value of the person in the present moment which is always filled with the opportunity of cutting through our conflicts and feeling the real concern we have for each other. I realized how so many of our basic relationships are threatened by our own impersonal attitudes, our concerns, jealousies, and hates. The frightening fact struck me that even in our caring for each other, providing for each other, living with each other, we can overlook the uncommunicative sense and breath of life, the silent loneliness that makes us what we are, that seeps down inside our lives, almost unaware, rooted into the center and depth of our personality and being.

Maybe the value of a bitter and painful loneliness is that in the intensity of the pain and feelings, we can come to realize our own worth in relation to another person. Through the feelings of loneliness, separation, guilt, fear, and helplessness in the face of death, I felt a deep relatedness to my mother, and through this came a feeling of warmth and compassion for others. She gave me a sense of the depths of the human being and human existence that can only be found through a close, personal relationship. I have come to understand how through anguish, pain and loneliness, a person could find the depths of himself and of another. In those moments with her, there was little time for hating, little time for conflict. All my energies were concentrated on the upsurge of warmth and concern and knowing of a personal love and the loneliness of standing within a relationship in the final moment. As at my birth, she gave me life, so in her death she gave me new life.

4.

He stood in the doorway of my office, a terribly stooped old man. Pain and misery, heavy wrinkles, lined his face. He stared beyond me, fiery, piercing eyes fixed to the floor, a face filled with indescribable loneliness and defeat. "Won't you come in and sit down?" I asked gently. He entered the room, but he did not sit. He began to pace, back and forth, back and forth. Increasingly, I felt the turbulence inside him which electrified my office with a kind of frozen tension. The tension mounted, becoming almost unbearable. Heavy beads of perspiration fell from his face and forehead. Tears filled his eyes. He started to speak several times but the words would not come. He stroked his hair roughly and pulled at his clothing. The pacing continued.

I felt his suffering keenly, deep inside me, spreading throughout my whole body. I remarked, "So utterly painful and lonely." "Lonely," he cried. "Lonely!" "Lonely!" he shouted, "I've been alone all my life." He spoke in rasping tones, his nerves drawn taut. "I've never been an honest person. I've never done anything I really wanted to do, nothing I truly believed in. I don't know what I believe in anymore. I don't know what I feel. I don't know what to do with myself. I wish I could die—how I have yearned, how I have longed for death to come, to end this misery. If I had the courage, I would kill myself. These headaches. I don't know how much more I can stand. I haven't slept for months. I wake up in the middle of the night. Everything is dark, black, ugly, empty. Right now my head is throbbing. I take pills. I try to rest. Nothing helps. My head is splitting. I don't think I can take this pain much longer. I wake with a start. My heart fills with terror. My wife and children are asleep, with me in the house—but I am entirely alone. I am not a father. I am not a husband. I'm no one. Look! See these tears. I could weep forever. Forever. I sometimes feel I cry for the whole world —a world that's sour and lost."

All this the old man uttered—sobbing, choking, sighing, gasping for breath. The sounds were thick. His tongue was fastened to his gums. Only with the greatest effort did he talk. It was almost unendurable. The lancinating physical pain and mental anguish mounted relentlessly. There was not even a moment of suspension so we could breathe normally and recapture our resources. His distress was cumulative, increasingly exhaustive.

In his completely weakened state, unknown urges, unknown capacities, a surprising strength enabled him to continue. From the beginning he had never been a real person. It was too late now, he felt. Nothing in life was real. For seventy-four years he had lived by other people's descriptions of him, others' perceptions of him. He had come to believe that this was his real self. He had become timid and shy when he might have discovered and developed social interests. He was silent when he might have something to say. He played cards every Tuesday and attended club meetings every Thursday when he might have enjoyed being alone, or conversing with his wife, or developing an avocation or hobby. He listened to the radio and watched television every evening when he might have discovered values in music and books. He did not know his real interests and talents, his real aspirations and goals. He never gave himself time to discover himself.

He asked in agony, "Do you know what it means not to feel anything, to be completely without feeling? Do you understand what it is to know only pain and loneliness? My family doesn't understand me. They think I have these headaches because my business is failing. They think I roam the house at night, moving from bed to couch to chair to floor, because I'm worrying about my business. They think I'm worrying about new possibilities and plans. So they soften me and treat me gingerly. Husband and father must have a quiet house, so the house is quiet. He must not be upset, so he is avoided. He must not be expected to be friendly and sociable because he is passive and shy. He must be indirectly talked into doing what they want, in the right way, at the right moment. It takes careful planning. He must have sympathy, even if it's false, to be able to face the tough, competitive world outside. They cannot and will not recognize that this man they handle with kid gloves, whom they fear upsetting, whom they decide has to be coddled and manipulated into buying new clothes, a new car, a new home, all the other possessions a family feels it must have, this man does not really exist and never did. But who is he? Can't you see? I do not really exist. I am nothing. Do you know what it is not to know how you feel, not to know your own thoughts, not to know what you believe, not to know what you want, not to be sure of anything but endless pain and suffering? And everyone else takes you for granted, on already formed opinions and actions, the same words, the same ways. How do I start to live again? I'm dying and I can't stop breathing. I can't stop living."

These were the themes of our talks together—self-denial, estrangement, rejection, excruciating pain, spreading loneliness. We met eight times. In each visit, his suffering and sense of isolation increased, reaching unbelievable heights. Often, I thought: "Surely this is it. He has reached the breaking point." He seemed at the very end of his power and resources. But he kept coming until I wondered whether I had not reached the breaking point. The only thing that kept me going was the certainty that without me there would be no one. I could not give up, abandon him, even when I questioned my own strength to continue to live through our conversations and the lonely terror not expressible in words. I suffered deeply in these hours with him. Each time he came I felt on the verge of sinking into total despair. Often when he wept, there were tears in my eyes too, and when his head ached painfully, I, too, felt the pain. When he paced and pulled at himself, I felt a terrible restlessness and agitation; when he was utterly alone and lonely, I was alone and lonely too. My full, complete presence was not enough to alleviate his suffering, his self-lacerating expressions. I felt an awful loneliness and desolation as I was not able to help him find a beginning, locate a direction, a new pathway of relatedness to himself and others. It hurt me deeply to see him grow increasingly, unbelievably tortured and not be able to help him find a meaning or even some beginning belief in the possibility of a good life. He was dying before me and something within me was dying too. I could not reach him. I do not know what effort of will power, what inner strivings of the heart, what forces kept me going in the face of this unendurable, mounting desolation, despair, and loneliness. I felt defeated and weakened, yet each time he came I met him squarely, honestly, directly. Each time my capacity for bearing with him seemed to be reaching a terminal point, new threads inside revived me. Somehow fresh strength flowed into me, mysteriously, encouraging me and enabling me to continue. I listened to him and believed in him. I was convinced he had the power within himself to find a new meaning in life. I continued to live with him in the crucial hours of psychic dying. My entire office filled with his aching. I could feel it everywhere in the room, in the floor, the walls, the furniture, the papers and books on my desk. It settled irrevocably and was stationary. For some time after he left, I did not move. I remained heavy as the feeling he left when he departed.

Then on the ninth appointment he did not come. What could this defection mean? How had I failed? Had he sensed my own growing struggle, my own exhaustion, my own loneliness? I searched within myself and within our relation but I could find no satisfactory answer.

Two weeks passed before he called. He spoke in a calm voice, in a totally different way from any previous words. "It's all so fresh and raw," he said, "and so new and startling that I'm constantly uncertain, but I feel I am coming into a totally new existence. I sometimes doubt that what I am feeling will last, but the feelings have persisted now almost two weeks and I'm beginning to recognize them as my own. I do not know what is happening or how, but by some strange miracle or inner working, I am beginning to breathe again and to live again. I do not want to see you just now because I must have further confirmation, but I will call you soon."

Six weeks later the old man came for the last time. I could barely recognize him. He looked youthful. His face was alive. His smile was radiant and so thrilling I felt tingling sensations everywhere inside me. He spoke warmly, confidently, "I came only to see your face light up, to be warmed by the gleam in your eyes. I know how much you suffered. I have seen your tortured face even after leaving you. I'll just sit here with you quietly a few minutes." So we sat in silence, each revelling in the birth, each warmed by a bond that emerged from deep and spreading roots in the hours of anguish and loneliness. We were no longer alone or lonely. We had found a new strength and sustenance in each other.

The fundamental communion in which we suffered enabled him to get to the very depths of his experience. Perhaps in arriving at the foundation of his grief and loneliness, immediate death or immediate life were the only choices within reach. He chose to live. From his rock bottom loneliness emerged a new life and a real self was restored.

III

CONCEPTS OF LONELINESS

The loneliness of modern life may be considered in two ways: the existential loneliness which inevitably is a part of human experience, and the loneliness of self-alienation and self-rejection which is not loneliness at all but a vague and disturbing anxiety.

Existential loneliness is an intrinsic and organic reality of human life in which there is both pain and triumphant creation emerging out of long periods of desolation. In existential loneliness man is fully aware of himself as an isolated and solitary individual while in loneliness anxiety man is separated from himself as a feeling and knowing person.

LONELINESS ANXIETY

Loneliness anxiety results from a fundamental breach between what one is and what one pretends to be, a basic alienation between man and man and between man and his nature.

Insidious fears of loneliness exist everywhere, nourished and fed by a sense of values and standards, by a way of life, which centers on acquisition and control. The emphasis on conformity, following directions, imitation, being like others, striving for power and status, increasingly alienates man from himself. The search for safety, order, and lack of anxiety through prediction and mastery eventually arouses inward feelings of despair and fears of loneliness. Unable to experience life in a genuine way, unable to relate authentically to his own nature and to other selves, the individual in Western culture often suffers from a dread of nothingness.

Why is it that so many individuals in modern life yearn for a fundamental relatedness to others but are unable to experience it? What is it that stands between man and man? Why is it that in face-to-face meetings man is unable to be spontaneous, truthful, direct with his fellow man? What makes so many people today act in opposition to their own natures, to their own desires and requirements? Why is self-estrangement and fear of loneliness so common in modern life? Margaret Wood in one of the few significant studies of loneliness, has asked, "What is there in us, or in the society of our time, that makes each of us a solitary individual, separate and apart, alone, yet needing others and needed by them?" [1]

Loneliness anxiety is a widespread condition in contemporary society. The individual no longer has an intimate sense of relatedness to the food he eats, the clothing he wears, the shelter which houses him. He no longer participates directly in the creation and production of the vital needs of his family and community. He no longer fashions with his own hands or from the desires of his heart. Modern man does not enjoy the companionship, support, and protection of his neighbors. He has been sharply cut off from primary groups and from family and kinship ties. He lives in an impersonal urban or suburban community where he meets others not as real persons but according to prescribed rules of conduct and prescribed modes of behavior. He strives to acquire the latest in comfort, convenience, and fashion. He works in a mechanized society, in which he is primarily a consumer, separated from any direct and personal contact with creation. Modern man is starving for communion with his fellow man and with other aspects of life and nature.

The fear of loneliness is an acute problem today because man has lost his world and he has lost his experience of neighborliness and community life. He experiences a feeling of alienation from the human world about him and he suffers from a corroding feeling of estrangement.[2]

Without intensive ties which have genuine meaning, modern man maintains an essential anonymity in society and in his community. Associations often are on a contractual basis and the person is treated as an object or thing or commodity. The individual fulfills his role in order to attain a higher reward, not because there is intrinsic value in being one's self, but because there is an economic value toward which

---

[1] Margaret M. Wood, *Paths of Loneliness* (New York: Columbia University Press, 1953), p. 3. Reprinted by permission of the publisher.

[2] Rollo May, Ernest Angel, and Henri F. Ellenberger, *Existence—A New Dimension in Psychiatry and Psychology* (New York: Basic Books, Inc., 1958).

one is directed. With advances in production, with the development of mechanical and automatic devices, with the change from rural to urban living, with the emphasis on making others' services indispensable, man has become increasingly competitive, exploitative, status conscious, and suspicious of his neighbor. He seeks group adjustment rather than group solidarity and enters into relations on the basis of formal agreements and contracts rather than trust. In modern life, much social interaction is between surface figures or ghosts rather than real persons.

Modern man lives without a personal world in which he has meaningful and enduring ties. The problem of this loss of world is not simply one of lack of interpersonal relations or lack of communion with one's fellows. Rollo May explains alienation, as follows:

> Underlying the economic, social and psychological aspects of alienation can be found a profound common denominator, namely, the alienation which is the ultimate consequence of four centuries of the outworking of the separation of man as subject from the objective world. This alienation has expressed itself for several centuries in Western man's passion to gain power over nature, but now shows itself in an estrangement from nature and a vague, unarticulated, and half-suppressed sense of despair of gaining any real relationship with the natural world, including one's own body.[3]

The separation of self from others and from nature constitutes the primary condition of loneliness anxiety in modern societies. The unhappiness, misery, fakery, pretense, the surface meetings, the failure to find genuine human contact often result in a fear and dread of loneliness.

Elder citizens in our society are particularly affected by the social and cultural changes and by the separation, urbanization, alienation, and automation in modern living. There is no longer a place for old age, no feeling of organic belonging, no reverence or respect or regard for the wisdom and talent of the ancient. Our elder citizens so often have feelings of uselessness, so often experience life as utterly futile. Old age is fertile soil for loneliness and the fear of a lonely old age far outweighs the fear of death in the thinking of many people.[4] Loss of friends and death of contemporaries are realities. The mourning and deep sense of loss are inevitable but the resounding and lasting depression which results and the emptiness and hopelessness are all a measure of the basic loneliness anxiety of our time.

Modern man is plagued with the vague, diffuse *fear* of loneliness. He

---

[3] *Ibid.*, p. 57. Reprinted by permission of Basic Books, Inc.
[4] Wingate M. Johnson, *The Years After Fifty* (New York: McGraw-Hill Book Co., Inc., 1947).

goes to endless measures, takes devious and circuitous pathways to avoid facing the experience of being lonely. Perhaps the loneliness of a meaningless existence, the absence of values, convictions, beliefs, and the fear of isolation are the most terrible kind of loneliness anxiety. This is the message in Balzac's *The Inventor's Suffering:*

> But learn one thing, impress it upon your mind which is still so malleable: man has a horror of aloneness. And of all kinds of aloneness, moral aloneness is the most terrible. The first hermits lived with God, they inhabited the world which is most populated, the world of the spirits. The first thought of man, be he a leper or a prisoner, a sinner or invalid, is: to have a companion of his fate. In order to satisfy this drive which is life itself, he applies all his strength, all his power, the energy of his whole life.

Loneliness anxiety in pathologic extremes is not rare in our society. It indicates a serious disturbance in health, often in the form of a bland existence. It is a type of chronic illness which debilitates the person and stifles any emergence of self or realization of capacities and talents. It is an exceedingly unpleasant, driving experience, resulting from inadequate fulfillment of the need for human intimacy—beginning in the early years with a failure to establish rich contact with the living, extending to the frustration of the need for tenderness and protective care, and into adult years when there is a failure to meet others on a genuine, fundamental, loving basis.

Frieda Fromm-Reichmann has made intensive studies of the psychiatric problems of loneliness anxiety based on her efforts to break through the loneliness she experienced from an inability and failure to communicate with schizophrenic patients, and the glorious moment when intimate contact was established. She relates one significant encounter with loneliness in the following passages.

> Perhaps my interest began with the young catatonic woman who broke through a period of completely blocked communication and obvious anxiety by responding when I asked her a question about her feeling miserable: She raised her hand with her thumb lifted, isolated from the four hidden fingers. I interpreted the signal with, "That lonely?," in a sympathetic tone of voice. At this, her facial expression loosened up as though in great relief and gratitude, and her fingers opened. Then she began to tell me about herself by means of her fingers, and she asked me by gestures to respond in kind. We continued with this finger conversation for one or two weeks, and as we did so, her anxious tension began to decrease and she began to break through her noncommunicative isolation; and subsequently she emerged altogether from her loneliness.[5]

[5] Frieda Fromm-Reichmann, "Loneliness," *Psychiatry*, Vol. 22 (1959), p. 1. Reprinted by permission of the publisher.

Is there any more heart-rending communication of panic than the terrifying feelings of loneliness expressed in the poem of a schizophrenic patient?

> And is there anyone at all?
>
> And is
> There anyone at all?
> I am knocking at the oaken door . . .
> And will it open
> Never now no more?
> I am calling, calling to you—
> Don't you hear?
> And is there anyone
> Near?
> And does this empty silence have to be?
> And is there no-one there at all
> To answer me?
>
> I do not know the road—
> I fear to fall
> And is there anyone
> At all? [6]

The emptiness of loneliness is revealed in this poem:

> No one comes near here
> Morning or night.
> The desolate grasses
> Grow out of sight.
> Only the wild hare
> Strays, then is gone.
> The Landlord is silence.
> The tenant is dawn. [7]

In these poems, it is obvious that the individuals felt sharply cut-off, drastically isolated and abandoned. They saw no hope at all in restoring a sense of relatedness, in communing with nature and other persons. They felt a complete absence of concern and love in the world.

Many individuals long fervently to be with others and to find love, but they are held back by their own restraining fears. Often accompanying this feeling of loneliness anxiety is a smoldering but helpless rage

---

[6] Eithne Tabor, *The Cliff's Edge: Songs of a Psychotic* (New York: Sheed & Ward Inc., 1950), pp. 9-10. Copyright © 1950 by Sheed & Ward Inc.; reprinted by permission of the publishers.

[7] Fromm-Reichmann, *op. cit.* (The author quoted a patient's poem, "Empty Lot,' by permission of the patient.) Reprinted by permission of the publisher.

and a desire for revenge for being "left out" of life. This feeling of be-ing cut-off and rejected is painully expressed by a young woman in psychotherapy:

> I always wanted her to love me and she never did. She always thought more of someone else than she did of me I never really pleased her because I did not have curly hair She thought more of others than she did of me She thought more of my cousin Mabel than she did of me She thought more of my sister than she did of me I cannot continue to care for people when they do not care for me My mother did not care for me She never believed in anything I did She did not even believe that I was sick She never cared that I was ill She did not care that I suffered so she did not care she never cared she never cared for me and I loved her so much I thought her so wonderful I thought her so beautiful She always seemed very beautiful to me but she never really loved me. If she had she would not have pushed me away when I came to kiss her good night If she had loved me she would not have done that She would have believed in me She would have cared when I was ill and suffered So but she didn't care She thought I deserved to be ill because I had done so many wrong things Everything I had ever done was wrong and my illness when I suffered so was my punishment for doing everything wrong She was not sorry She did not care She was glad She was glad I suffered so She laughed at my suffering I knew she laughed though I did not really see her but I knew she laughed I lay in bed and suffered so and she was glad and laughed at me and I came to hate her because I loved her so much and she never cared for me I hated her and wished to kill her I would have killed her if I could because she never cared for me.[8]

The chronically lonely person sometimes sends out appeals for friend-ship and a mate. Lonely hearts clubs and similar organizations are a product of twentieth century society and twentieth century loneliness anxiety. Thousands of lost and hungry souls appeal to these organiza-tions which promise, "Somewhere a voice is calling—calling to you." In a scathing critique of these groups, Steiner writes:

> Most of the advertising sent out by the Clubs are masterpieces of double-talk, creating the impression that this is a guaranteed method of solving one's loneliness. Close scrutiny reveals, however, that they actually say only that they understand their business and know how to conduct it.[9]

A story of the failure of a "lonely hearts" marriage was reported in *The Detroit Free Press* (August 18, 1959). The headline read: *"Brought*

---

[8] Karl Menninger, *Love Against Hate* (New York: Harcourt, Brace & Co., 1942), p. 156. Copyright © 1942 by Karl Menninger and Jeanetta Lyle Menninger; re-printed by permission of Harcourt, Brace & World, Inc.

[9] Lee Steiner, *Where Do People Take Their Troubles?* (Boston: Houghton Mifflin Co. 1945). p. 105. Reprinted by permission of the author.

Together In Loneliness, Oldsters Part In Bitterness." The story continues:

> A lonely widower. A lonely widow. A "lonely hearts" listing. A marriage.
> A divorce—just two years later. . . . They lived as man and wife until
> a year ago, and since only have lived in the same house. In granting a
> divorce, the judge said, "This is the same old story. Two elderly lonely
> people thrown together, each in the hope they would improve their lot.
> You couldn't find two more clashing personalities anywhere. The only
> thing they had in common was loneliness. Lonely hearts magazines are
> fiendish devices." [10]

Feelings of inferiority are also connected with loneliness anxiety.
Great pain and suffering is provoked by a feeling of being unloved and
neglected. Thomas Wolfe described these torturing feelings of inferiority when he wrote:

> Forever and forever in our loneliness, shameful feelings of inferiority
> will rise up suddenly to overwhelm us in a poisonous flood of horror,
> disbelief, and desolation, to sicken and corrupt our health and confidence,
> to spread pollution at the very root of strong, exultant joy.[11]

In attempting to overcome loneliness anxiety, the individual sometimes gives up his individuality and submerges himself in dependency
relations. Fromm explains why such a solution to standing alone in the
face of a perilous and powerful world inevitably fails.

> Just as a child can never return to the mother's womb physically, so it
> can never reverse, psychically, the process of individuation. Attempts to do
> so necessarily assume the character of submission, in which the basic
> contradiction between the authority and the child who submits to it is
> never eliminated. Consciously the child may feel secure and satisfied, but
> unconsciously it realizes that the price it pays is giving up strength and the
> integrity of its self. Thus the result of submission is the very opposite
> of what it was to be: submission increases the child's insecurity and at
> the same time creates hostility and rebelliousness, which is the more
> frightening since it is directed against the very persons on whom the
> child has remained or become dependent.[12]

The person suffering from loneliness anxiety is deeply suspicious.
Even the slightest criticism hurts him. He often perceives nonexistent
deprecation in surface or tangential remarks. Because he feels such
grave failure in everything he undertakes, because he constantly strives

---

[10] Reprinted by permission of *The Detroit Free Press* from an unsigned article of
August 18, 1959.

[11] Thomas Wolfe, *The Hills Beyond* (New York: Harper & Brothers, 1941), p. 184.

[12] Erich Fromm, *Escape From Freedom* (New York: Holt, Rinehart and Winston,
Inc., 1941), p. 29. Reprinted by permission of the publishers.

to raise his level of achievement and win praise and approval and at the same time employs devices and strategies which constantly alienate him from others, eventually he either gives up or responds with aggression to cover up his inner feeling of separation, anxiety, and despair. He is not open enough, flexible enough, expansive enough to attach himself to new persons and find value in new experiences. If he could only surrender to his real loneliness, he might emerge as a new person.

Aggressiveness often is a disguise of loneliness anxiety and may be expressed as cynicism and contempt for love and cultural interests. When glorification for the predatory elements in the world is broken, the person reveals a horrible loneliness and a passionate desire to be loved by other people and to belong to them. Loneliness anxiety is a defense against an unloving world, the pain of isolation, and the yearning for tenderness and security. Underneath this defense, the individual reveals an excessive and repressed sentimentality and experiences immense anxiety that his weakness will be exposed.

Much of the loneliness anxiety in our society is not the psychiatric loneliness which results from rejection or abandonment in childhood. It is possible to live too much in the world, to try to escape loneliness by constant talk, by surrounding one's self with others, by modeling one's life from people in authority or with high status. Alienated from his own self, the individual does not mean what he says and does not do what he believes and feels. He learns to respond with surface or approved thoughts. He learns to use devious and indirect ways, and to base his behavior on the standards and expectations of others. Cut-off from his own self, he is unable to have communal experiences with others, though he may be popular, or to experience a sense of relation with nature. Many of these individuals love truth, yet their lives are predicated on appearances and false ties; they do not concentrate their energies enough to be able to become in fact what they are in inspiration. Literally millions of adults who are protected and loved, who experienced intimate relations in their early years, suffer the consequences of an impersonal, competitive world of self-denial and alienation. They often go to great lengths to escape or overcome the fear of loneliness, to avoid any direct or genuine facing of their own inner experience. What is it that drives man to surround himself with the same external double-talk, the same surface interests and activities during his evenings at home as during his days at work?[13] It is the terror of loneliness, not

---

[13] David Riesman, Reuel Denney, and Nathan Glazer, *The Lonely Crowd* (New Haven, Conn.: Yale University Press, 1950), pp. 170-171.

loneliness itself but loneliness anxiety, the fear of being left alone, of being left out. It is absolutely necessary to keep busy, active, have a full schedule, be with others, escape into the fantasies, dramas, and lives of others on television or in the movies. Everything is geared toward filling and killing time to avoid feeling the emptiness of life and the vague dissatisfactions of acquiring possessions, gaining status and power, and behaving in the appropriate and approved ways. The escape from loneliness is actually an escape from facing the fear of loneliness.

Cultural interests and activities and community pursuits provide a powerful antidote to the fear of loneliness. But all the while, the person experiences loneliness in a vague and undifferentiated form—the loneliness anxiety of feeling alone even in a crowd, of talking incessantly with others while not saying anything meaningful or productive, of discussing the same subjects in the same ways in different groups— the loneliness anxiety of being a member of a club or organization without any true identity or relatedness to others, of acquisition without satisfaction—the anxiety of consuming where there is no essential tie to creating—the anxiety created when real desires and interests are abandoned in favor of social, economic, and vocational rewards. The other directed person is a lonely person who tries to assuage his loneliness in the crowd, in the poker game in the back room with its praise of masks, at cocktail parties afternoon and night.[14] Whyte has shown how the attempt to overcome loneliness in suburban life extends to the planning of houses.

> All other things being equal—and it is amazing how much all other things are equal in suburbia—it would appear that certain kinds of physical layouts can virtually produce the "happy" group. To some the moral would seem simplicity itself. Planners can argue that if they can find what it is that creates cohesiveness it would follow that by deliberately building these features into the new housing they could at once eliminate the loneliness of modern life.[15]

Efforts of this kind result in a sick loneliness, the loneliness of fakery and pretense, the loneliness of the calculated and contrived, the loneliness of a ready-made solution replacing the satisfaction of creating with one's own talents, capacities, and skills.

One does not combat loneliness with plans which aim to create an aura of friendliness. Efforts to deceive the individual by the subtle and

[14] *Ibid.*
[15] William H. Whyte, Jr., *The Organization Man* (New York: Simon and Schuster, Inc., 1956), p. 348. Copyright © 1956 by William H. Whyte, Jr.; reprinted by permission of the publishers.

invisible emanation of neighborliness, to surround him with an atmosphere of community fellowship through arrangement of color and de-
sign, only accentuate the emptiness of life. Contrived cheerfulness,
warmth, and invitation register deep down as superficial openness and
leave the person feeling that there is no genuine way to establish roots
with others. If other-directed people could discover how much meaningless work they do, if they could see that they can no more assuage their
loneliness in a crowd of peers or by manipulating the environment than
one can mitigate one's thirst by drinking sea water, then we might expect them to become more attentive to their own real feelings and aspirations, to realize the significance of their own real lives, and to
search for genuine relatedness with others and with nature.[16]

EXISTENTIAL LONELINESS

In contrast to the loneliness anxiety of modern life is the inevitable,
real loneliness of genuine experience. Thomas Wolfe regarded loneliness as an intrinsic condition of existence.

> The whole conviction of my life now rests upon the belief that
> loneliness, far from being a rare and curious phenomenon, peculiar to
> myself and to a few other solitary men, is the central and inevitable fact
> of human existence. . . . All this hideous doubt, despair, and dark con-
> fusion of the soul a lonely man must know, for he is united to no image
> save that which he creates himself, he is bolstered by no other knowledge
> save that which he can gather for himself with the vision of his own eyes
> and brain. He is sustained and cheered and aided by no party, he is
> given comfort by no creed, he has no faith in him except his own. And
> often that faith deserts him, leaving him shaken and filled with impotence.
> And then it seems to him that his life has come to nothing, that he is
> ruined, lost, and broken past redemption, and that morning—bright,
> shining morning, with its promise of new beginnings—will never come
> upon the earth again as it did once.[17]

Wolfe believed that loneliness is an essential condition of creativity,
that out of the depths of grief, despair, and the shattering feeling of total impotency springs the urge to create new forms and images and to
discover unique ways of being aware and expressing experience.

The vastness of life itself produces the emotional climate of existential loneliness, the mystery of a new dawn, the endless stretches of sea

[16] Reisman, *et al., op. cit.,* p. 373.
[17] Wolfe, *op. cit.,* pp. 186, 189.

and sky, the immense impact of air, and time, and space, the unfathomable workings of the universe. The constant, everlasting weather of man's life is not love but loneliness. Love is the rare and precious flower but loneliness pervades each new day and each new night.

The deepest experiences the soul can know—the birth of a baby, the prolonged illness or death of a loved relative, the tortuous pain or the isolation of disease, the creation of a poem, a painting, a symphony, the grief of a fire, a flood, an accident—each in its own way touches upon the roots of loneliness. In all these experiences we must perforce go alone.

The inevitability of the lonely heart is expressed in the following poem:

> Sometimes I wonder what will become of me
> My heart yearns for permanence which never can be
> I do not know a real face any more
> And my compassion is misplaced
> The spontaneity and joy and continuity are gone
> Where is the beginning which remains
> Where is the heart which speaks only truth
> No where, no more, will I find commitment to meet mine
> To live a lie, to die of life, to search in failure
> Is this to be my destiny?

It takes creative courage to accept the inevitable, existential loneliness of life, to face one's essential loneliness openly and honestly. It requires inner fortitude not to be afraid or overwhelmed with the fear of being and the fear of being alone.

The experience of separation or isolation is not unhealthy any more than any condition of human existence is unhealthy. Ultimately each man is alone but when the individual maintains a truthful self-identity, such isolation is strengthening and induces deeper sensitivities and awareness. In contrast, self-alienation and estrangement drive one to avoid separation. The fear of loneliness is a sickness which promotes dehumanization and insensitivity. In the extreme, the person stops feeling altogether and tries to live solely by rational means and cognitive directions. This is the terrible tragedy of modern life—the alienation of man from his own feelings, the desensitization of man to his own suffering and grief, the fear of man to experience his own loneliness and pain and the loneliness and misery of others.

Loneliness is as much organic to human existence as the blood is to the heart. It is a dimension of human life whether existential, sociological, or psychological, whatever its derivatives or forms, whatever its history, it is a reality of life. Its fear, evasion, denial, and the accompanying attempts to escape the experience of being lonely will forever isolate the person from his own existence, will afflict and separate him from his own resources so that there is no development, no creative emergence, no growth in awareness, perceptiveness, sensitivity. If the individual does not exercise his loneliness, one significant capacity and dimension of being human remains undeveloped, denied. A fear of despair, an agony of aloneness replaces the real experience but strategies of escape and alienation can never substitute for the growth-inducing, deepening values of a genuine, vital, lonely experience.

Loneliness has a developmental history beginning in infancy, when the need for contact is temporarily unresolved, and continuing through the need for ultimate relatedness. It enters into crucial periods of development and critical experiences in childhood and reaches full significance in preadolescence. Sullivan[18] traced the various motivational systems in human development which enter into the experience of real loneliness. The first is the need for contact—tenderness and protective care in infancy and the early years. These needs extend into childhood when components of what will ultimately be experienced as loneliness appear in the need for adult participation in activities. When the child cannot obtain adult presence and participation, loneliness results. The child attempts to assuage the feeling of isolation by entering into a rich fantasy life, and by engaging in imaginary personifications. The greater the intensity of separation, the greater the development of his sense of social isolation and parental rejection. Each person as he grows experiences a sense of separation as a natural challenge to the development of individuality. This sense of isolation is dramatically felt by the child. Because of his inability to take care of himself in the all-important functions, communication with others is a matter of life and death for him. The possibility of being abandoned or left alone is the most serious threat to the child's whole existence.[19] Of the many kinds of temporary abandonment, no experience is more desolating to a child than having to be in a hospital alone. The cold marble floors; the impersonal rules and regulations; the extreme bleak whiteness everywhere; the desensitized atmosphere; the neat, empty categorical arrangement of food and beds, external to the individual child and his personal preferences; the

[18] Harry Stack Sullivan, *The Interpersonal Theory of Psychiatry* (New York: W. W. Norton & Co., Inc., 1953), pp. 260-262.
[19] Fromm, *op. cit.*

constant checks and routines; the frequent medication and shots which he does not comprehend; the disrespect for the integrity of his wishes and interests; the absence of genuine human warmth; and the presence of surface voices, surface smiles, and superficial words and meetings; all enter into the loneliness of hospital life.

For years medical people have known that hospitalization may do a child more harm than good—not only in contributing to his sense of abandonment, but in the development of terrifying fears, anxiety, and traumas which survive long after the physical defect has been rectified. Knowing the significance of emotional factors in the etiology of physical disease and in the development of health, doctors and nurses have made efforts to reach the child, sympathetically expressing concern for his pain, being more gentle, giving information, and sometimes even allowing the child to set the pace. But most children see through this kind of behavior when it is mere role-playing or rank professionalism. This kind of surface behavior is easily distinguished by the child from the spontaneous feelings of the heart. Furthermore, even the genuine feelings of a nurse or physician can never reach deeply enough to substitute for the love embedded in the child's relationship with his mother or father. The nurse or doctor can never give him a feeling of safety and the strength to face the severe trial of a painful illness.

Why is it that hospitals continue to move mothers and fathers "out of the way" when scientific evidence is now available affirming the vital nature of the mother's presence in restoring the child to health. The mother is certainly significant as a curative agent and sometimes absolutely crucial to the child's recovery.

Contrary to previous beliefs, parents do not, as a rule, interfere with hospital procedures, and, on the contrary, can assist the hard-pressed staff and greatly aid the child in recovery from the trauma of hospitalization and from operative conditions. In the hospital, as in the home, the emotional anchorage of the mother offers many assets for recovery and for healthy emotional growth.

Harold, for example, showed regression in many aspects of his behavior when he had his tonsillectomy at the hospital. The anxiety he suffered in being able to see his mother only in the evening precipitated his regression and made his convalescence during and after hospitalization more difficult and prolonged than it might have been. In Harold's case, the practice of the hospital in advising his parents not to remain with him before and after the operation literally severed him from the anchorage he so desperately needed during his emotionally traumatic experience.[20]

With evidence consistently pointing to the necessity of mother and child remaining together during a crisis, why does the hospital insist on separating them? Why, with the evidence showing that the individual knows himself better than anyone else, is the child in the hospital so ignored and mistrusted? Why, when we have learned through serious mistakes that in an authoritarian atmosphere, children rebel at the first opportunity, or submit to the point of total self-denial, do most hospitals continue to operate with the discipline of an army barracks in wartime?

When a child is in terror in a hospital, he needs his parents in every painful experience to help him bear the loneliness of living with strangers who often apparently care more about X-rays, charts, and shots, and temperatures, and tests, than they do about him. There is no one, absolutely no one, who can comfort the child, and give him the strength to face his ordeal except his mother or father or some person to whom he is significantly related. Instead of making a place available for parents where they can participate and share in the child's fears and pains, all sorts of devices are used to extricate parents, not only from the room but in accompanying a child when he must face the terrible ordeals of X-rays and other tests. The many strangers who are part of these procedures rarely have any concern for the individual child. One thing is certain, if a parent decides to stay with his child through every one of these frightening procedures, no amount of pressure on the part of hospital staff can evict the parent. But when the parent leaves the child alone to face hospital tests and hospital strangers, the parent cannot know what horrors the child may be subjected to and what emotional lacerations will be inflicted upon him. The parent cannot answer when the child cries out in distress.

Every child who is significantly related to his mother or father requires the presence of the parent in every important experience in the hospital until he himself decides he is able to be alone. No amount of dictation or persuasion on the part of nurses or doctors should cause the parent to abandon the child. In this respect, Dr. Alvarez comments:

> One of the cruelest things we do in America is to send a child up to the operating room all by himself. The mother should go with the child at least up to the operating-room floor, where, perhaps in a special room,

---

[20] Max L. Hutt and Robert G. Gibby, *Child: Development and Adjustment* (Englewood Cliffs, N. J.: Allyn & Bacon, 1959).

the child could be anesthetized while the mother is present. Then the sleeping child could be wheeled into the operating room.

As I have said before, it is time that hospital authorities began to think of these things. They ought to realize that when parents and children are left with very distressing memories of what happened in the hospital, this does not make for good public relations.[21]

The parents' presence not only contributes positively to the child's sense of security and confidence, which are certainly vital ingredients in his recovery, but also enables him to continue to be an individual with unique interests and unique ways. Parents are able to help the child continue to grow by providing time and resources, while hospital staffs, with so many pressing responsibilities, cannot become genuinely concerned with the individual child and his interests, wishes, and needs.

When a child asks a question, he has a right to an answer and he has a right to the truth—simple, direct, forthright. After all, he wants to know what is being done to him and why. The information will enable him to accept the treatment. He can accept much more fully what he can understand.

The loneliness which the child experiences even when the parent is present is painful enough because in the end there are certain experiences which the child must face alone. There are times when he will realize how alone he is as an individual. This is the inevitable loneliness of human existence. But when the child is abandoned, his terror lives inside. He will always remember the lonely, isolated hours of abandonment. He feels that if his parents really loved and cared for him they would not have left him to face his pain alone.

However appealing the arguments of the physician or nurse may be, as long as the child requires it, the parent must remain or answer for the consequences of a severe traumatic experience for the child. When our daughter, Wendy, was in the hospital for an emergency overnight visit, she deeply wanted her mother to remain. The nurse used every trick to persuade Wendy that her mother's presence was not essential. The hospital could provide for all her needs. Wendy remained adamant. She needed her mother standing by to help her live through the fear and the pain. Finally, in desperation, the nurse said, "But everytime you want something all you need do is to ring this buzzer and the nurse will come." Wendy answered immediately, "If I wake up at night and cry and call for my Momma, I want her here. The buzzer cannot bring her to me." Wendy's mother stayed. Wendy woke up several times and

[21] Reprinted from Dr. Walter C. Alvarez's column of June 9, 1959 by permission of *The Register and Tribune Syndicate* of Des Moines, Iowa.

called. Her mother was there to comfort her and give her sustenance. And when a child calls and the mother is not there to answer, then what terrors does the child experience in his heart? This terror of the heart is something a person can understand only if he opens himself to it. Every nurse and doctor would want the parent to remain if he knew the meaning of the child's desperate existence when he lay in bed at night, terrified and alone.

THE LONELY EXPERIENCE[22]

In all my thirteen years I have only been lonely once, that is really lonely. When I was seven years old I cut my hand on broken glass. I went to the doctor and from there to the hospital with some severed tendons.

I wasn't at all bothered. I thought it would be a real "blast."

I was happy when I got my bed in the girls' section on the childrens' ward, and when I met my neighbors who were twins (both eight years old) and having their tonsils removed. I was happy when they wheeled me into the operating room. I wasn't too sad even when they gave me that awful ether and I went to "Sleepville, U.S.A."

I was happy throughout the day. After all Mom and Dad were there, the girls next door were nice, the T.V. worked, and I had a real "cool" cast to show off to all the kids.

It wasn't until I discovered I was to spend the night alone at the hospital that I realized it wasn't going to be all fun.

That night after Mom and Dad were gone and everyone was sleeping I experienced loneliness for the first time in my life.

I yelled for the nurse. She brought me ice-water and a sedative of some sort to put me to sleep. Of course it didn't work. That night I sat up in bed 'till about midnight when the nurse came in and told me that my mother had called and asked about me. The nurse told her I was asleep (the liar).

The night dragged on and on and I was absolutely miserable. The cracks in the wall became monsters. It was one o'clock A.M. when I began to wonder where Mom was. She was to get me at 10:00 A.M.

The night was a lonely nightmare. I spent every second of it sitting, fretting, tossing, turning, crying to myself, and yelling "Nurse!" To

---

[22] The illustrations in this chapter are taken from actual situations, either directly from my own experience or from the experience of others, conveyed to me in written or spoken form.

make things worse I didn't like the nurse and there was no one awake to talk to (except a stupid boy in the boys' ward). Now I feel sorry for him, he must have been lonely too.

When Mom finally came I forgot how terribly lonely I was. I forgot just how bad it was until now six years later, when you gave us this opportunity to tell our experiences of loneliness.

I am afraid the only effect or mark that night left on me was bad. Now I am scared stiff of hospitals.

Feelings of loneliness must often be hidden in childhood. They are too frightening and disturbing—like any intense, severe, disturbing emotion these feelings must be curbed, controlled, denied, or, if expressed, quickly resolved or eliminated through busy activities and goals. One aspect of this "cover up" campaign is that we make our children feel that "nice" people have only "nice" emotions.[23] Children become afraid early to let others know how they actually feel. The natural and inevitable loneliness resulting in childhood must be distorted and controlled in interactions with others. The child soon believes he can show his parents only an expurgated, carefully edited version of his inner life. He begins to suffer deep feelings of guilt and inadequacy as he learns to regard his loneliness as "bad" and as a kind of sickness. The natural loneliness of inner life becomes confounded and confused, and sometimes the child enters into the tragic loneliness anxiety of self-alienation. For this reason it is important to give children an opportunity to express their experiences of loneliness. It is one way to break through the terrible sense of guilt and isolation. The following essays provided such an opportunity for a group of preadolescent youngsters. In these essays, the very core of the lonely experience is captured.

1.

Empty, that's how it feels to be lonely. A sense of being in a deep dark pit, with nothing in sight, and no way out. It feels like a dark rainy day. Just there, just sitting there lonely. It's like a blue, a dark blue, almost a black, but then it's also a light blue, washed out and dingy. It's a deep empty pit in your stomach.

[23] Bonaro W. Overstreet, *Understanding Fear in Ourselves and Others* (New York: Harper & Brothers, 1951).

Loneliness brings thinking. When lonely I feel like thinking. Not anything special, just thinking—

Loneliness leaves some aftereffects. Mostly just a tired feeling. Not wanting to talk to anyone, not wanting to do anything. But, most of them can be remedied by just starting to do something. Something that you like to do.

2.

When loneliness strikes I feel thoroughly abandoned.

To me loneliness seems to have different stages. At first I usually feel somewhat mad, even a little bitter toward the person who caused my loneliness. Many things pass through my mind when I'm lonely. After a while I sometimes begin to wonder—is our friendship really worth these countless, tormenting hours?

It seems almost as though a transparent barrier has separated my world from that of my friend. A barrier too high to scale and too solid to get through. Therefore I'm a captive of loneliness until it chooses to release me.

To me it seems that loneliness is sort of a cunning thing. It kind of knows "torture" methods of its own. Sometimes it can begin to convince you that false truths are right, or it can let you see your friends having fun without you, and that can hurt.

After I have been lonely for some time things usually start to reason out. Gradually loneliness loosens its grip completely and everything is fine again.

3.

Loneliness as described in the dictionary means without company lonely. I believe that it goes a lot deeper than just lonely, or withou company.

In the loneliness that I am going to tell about it was mostly an empty feeling, a feeling that I was not wanted, even though I was a member of a group.

I was in the sixth grade and I was in a small group of girls. Most people call this a clique. We had parties every weekend with the same boys and girls, never letting any outsiders in. But we did let some out or shall I say kick them out. We took one girl and made the going rough for her until she finally had to drop out of the clique.

I saw how much this girl was hurt and decided never to do anything like that again to anybody.

When the group tried to kick another girl out I was against it and I guess it showed because gradually I was scorned by the girls too and shoved out of the group.

Naturally I was hurt and lonely but I couldn't do much about it. Through this experience I have witnessed and felt that horrible feeling of loneliness. I have profited from this experience. My beliefs now are different. I try to act human to everybody and not just to a few girls in a clique.

4.

It was a terrible experience.

This is the way I would describe how I felt when my best boy-friend moved.

Up until this point in my life, he seemed to be the only *real* friend I had—oh, I had other boy-friends, but to me, he seemed just like a brother.

The period from the day he left to about a week after was about the worst for me. I felt that life was all over for me, and there seemed to be nothing to look forward to.

Nothing seemed to go right for me, and I felt that no one in the world could possibly be as lonely as I was.

I was beginning to hope that the world would come to an end.

—I didn't care.

5.

Slowly I walked up and down the room. The house was empty. A pang of loneliness came over me. I felt small and alone looking at the deep blue of the sky. The shadows of the willow coated the ground in black. Loneliness, not a new feeling, seemed to come like a shadow with the setting sun. The melancholy scene filled me with the longing for someone, anyone. Time seemed suspended. No sound broke the silence of the evening. I was completely shut off from the world. Then from out of nowhere there came the sound of a motor and light broke through the colorless scene. A car slowly turned up the driveway, allowing time to go on and the sun to set.

These experiences of loneliness are not rare. They are realities which children face every year—happenings beyond human control or prediction. Which of us has not known the child alone at home, temporarily abandoned by his parents, the child without friends and with "nothing to do," the child sent away to camp or school, the child who feels completely isolated in the group, the child who feels his parents do not love him or who feels they care more for his brother or sister, the child who is not recognized or chosen at school, the one who is usually left out, the child who faces an overnight or lengthy hospitalization, the child in a new school or a new neighborhood, the child who walks to and from school alone, the child facing a new school year without friends, the child whose pals reject him or turn against him, the child condemned by his parents, forced to stay alone in his room as punishment. These are situations which nearly every child faces at some time in his life, but they do not necessarily defeat or alienate him. These experiences of loneliness have potential value and are a way to learning and to a new life.

Riesman has forcefully shown how inner-directed children suffer a fate of loneliness both in and outside the home where there may be frequent hazing, persecution, and misunderstanding. He says the adult rarely offers sympathy or guidance to the lonely child. Often these children are even unaware that they have rights to friendship, understanding, or agreeable play. They are unaware that adults may be interested in such matters. They often suffer in silence. Riesman sees advantages of loneliness, as the following excerpt shows.

> We can see that in a society which values inner-direction, loneliness and even persecution are not thought of as the worst of fates. . . . While adults seldom intervene to guide or help the lonely child, neither do they tell him that he should be a part of a crowd and must have fun.[24]

Thus the lonely child is left alone, free of many of the usual pressures for conformity. Regarded as strange or peculiar, perceived as an isolate, he is free to experience his existential loneliness, to exercise and actualize this capacity and in the process to become sensitive and aware of the world in a deep and meaningful way.

Loneliness is a creative experience when it emerges naturally from the individual self. This is well documented. The person who stands out in literature, music, art, science is often a lonely individual. He realizes

[24] Riesman, et al., op. cit., pp. 68-69.

creative forms through his own self. The lonely voyager, the mountain
climber, the seafarer, the explorer, the inventor, all know moments of
deep, unforgettable loneliness. In expressing one's uniqueness, the person often appears to others as peculiar, different, deviant, and sometimes
even bizarre. It is terribly lonely to be misunderstood, wrongly in-
terpreted, falsely analyzed, to be impugned with evil motives. Being different, standing out in a group is often regarded as a sign of psycho-social
illness. More and more the individual who stands alone, even though of
high ideals and constructive values, may be forced to isolate himself or
to struggle for society's acceptance of him as a unique person. In expressing his sense of inner truth, the creative person must often experience a desolate and lonely existence. This was the nature of the experience of a young man in psychotherapy who was trying to maintain his
idiosyncratic perceptions.

> . . . and then sometimes I (*pause*), I don't know if this makes sense,
> but . . . sometimes I just feel that . . . I want to exist, so to speak, com-
> pletely . . . within myself, I mean, within . . . without any . . . social
> intercourse . . . And then (*sighs*) at other times I feel that I don't want
> to exist within myself at all because it . . . brings sort of agony or torment
> or sort of mental . . . hardships. And then I just want to . . . indulge in
> complete . . . normal . . . social . . . relationships, and I don't want at
> all to exist within myself . . . But, as I said . . . I mean, deep within my-
> self, I feel that it has to be. I mean, no external assurance would really
> alter anything or . . . would make any modification or . . . well, I mean,
> it has to be of some . . . some inner realization or inner awareness of just
> what I am. (*Pause*) . . . But I think the most important thing . . . is the
> fact . . . I feel that . . . well, that I realize that . . . the people of . . .
> I mean, the judgment of other people . . . outside yourself is not really
> . . . important. And you can only realize your own value . . . I mean
> through some inner awareness of what you feel that you are. And no matter
> what other people think of it, it makes really no difference unless you
> . . . you, yourself, feel that way about . . . if you don't agree with them,
> then you . . . it just just won't (*sighs*) just won't help any . . . I feel that
> participation and things like that would only be meant toward this and
> that . . . coming to depend more upon yourself. (*Pause*) Well, I mean,
> not depend on yourself to the extent that you exclude, I mean, human
> relations or anything like that. (*Pause*) Just depend on yourself so that
> (*pause*) you realize that you (*pause*) do have the . . . potentialities, I mean,
> of doing something, instead of having to ask people all the time whether
> they think it's right or not.[25]

[25] Carl R. Rogers and Rosalind F. Dymond, *Psychotherapy and Personality Change*
(Chicago: The University of Chicago Press, 1954), pp. 349-409. Copyright © 1954
by the University of Chicago; reprinted by permission of the publisher.

The books of the Old Testament provide a profound and powerful literature, a supreme history of man's loneliness. The terrible feeling of abandonment and isolation, the scourge of being forsaken, the loneliness of being destroyed without cause are beautifully portrayed in the sacred verse of *Job*.

Let the day perish wherein I was born and the night *in which* it was said, There is a man child conceived.

Let that day be darkness; let not God regard it from above, neither let the light shine upon it.

Let darkness and the shadow of death stain it; let a cloud dwell upon it; let the blackness of the day terrify it.

As for that night, let darkness seize upon it; let it not be joined unto the days of the year, let it not come into the number of the months.

Lo, let that night be solitary, let no joyful voice come therein.

Let them curse it that curse the day, who are ready to raise up their mourning. . . .

Why died I not from the womb? *why* did I *not* give up the ghost when I came out of the belly? . . .

Wherefore is light given to him that is in misery, and life unto the bitter *in* soul.

Which long for death, but it *cometh* not; and dig for it meantime for hid treasures;

Which rejoice exceedingly, *and* are glad, when they can find the grave?

Why is light given to a man whose way is hid, and whom God had hedged in?

For my sighing cometh before I eat, and my roarings are poured out like waters. . . .

Oh that my grief were weighted, and my calamity laid in the balances together!

For now it would be heavier than the sand of the sea: therefore my words are swallowed up.

Alienated from his friends, from all intimate human contact, cut off from his fields, his animals, his home, his family, Job makes a final appeal, supplicates God to help him understand why he has been wronged, to help him see the reasons for his calamities. He craves pity, sympathy, affirmation as he bemoans his unjust fate.

Behold, I cry out of wrong, but I am not heard: I cry aloud, but *there is* no judgment. . . .

He hath stripped me of my glory, and taken the crown *from* my head.

He hath destroyed me on every side, and I am gone: and mine hope hath he removed like a tree. . . .

My kinsfolk have failed and my familiar friends have forgotten me.

They that dwell in mine house, and my maids, count me for a stranger: I am an alien in their sight.

I called my servant, and he gave *me* no answer; I entreated him with my
mouth.
My breath is strange to my wife, though I entreated for the children's
sake of mine own body.
Yea young children despised me: I arose, and they spake against me.
All my inward friends abhorred me: and they whom I loved are turned
against me. . . .
Have pity upon me, have pity upon me, O Ye my friends; for the hand of
God hath touched me. . . .[26]

Many of the Hebrew prayers in the Yom Kippur service enable the
person to overcome the loneliness of estrangement, the isolating consequence of committing evil. A moving search for peace, harmony, relatedness, love, and identity with God is contained in lamentations from the
Conclusion Service, as in the following prayer:

O may our prayers come before thee, and withdraw not thyself from our
supplications, for we are not so shameless of face, or hardened, as to
declare in thy presence, O Eternal, our God and the God of our fathers,
that we are righteous, and have not sinned; verily (we confess) we have
sinned.
We have trespassed, we have dealt treacherously, we have stolen, we have
spoken slander, we have committed iniquity, and have done wickedly;
we have acted presumptuously; we have committed violence; we have
framed falsehood; we have counselled evil; we have uttered lies; we have
scorned; we have rebelled; we have blasphemed; we have revolted; we
have acted perversely; we have transgressed; we have oppressed; we
have been stiff-necked; we have acted wickedly; we have corrupted; we
have done abominably, we have gone astray, and have caused others to
err; we have turned aside from thy excellent precepts and institutions,
and which hath not profited us; but thou art just concerning all that is
come upon us; for thou hast dealt most truly, but we have done wickedly.[27]

The sermons of *Ecclesiastes* support the value of human loneliness,
cogently point out the natural state of sorrow, and show the relationship between increasing knowledge and wisdom and increasing loneliness.

I communed with mine own heart, saying Lo I am come to great estate,
and have gotten more wisdom, than all *they* that have been before me in
Jerusalem: Yea my heart had great experience of wisdom and knowledge.
And I gave my heart to know wisdom, and to know madness and folly:
I perceived that this also is vexation of spirit.

[26] London and Foreign Bible Society, *The Holy Bible* (London: Eyre and Spottiswoods, Ltd.).
[27] *Form of Prayers for the Day of Atonement*, rev. ed., English trans. (New York:
Hebrew Publishing Co.).

> For in much wisdom *is* much grief: and he that increaseth knowledge increaseth sorrow.
>
> To every *thing there is* a season, and a time to every purpose under the heaven:
>
> A time to be born, and a time to die; a time to plant, and a time to pluck up *that which is* planted;
>
> A time to kill, and a time to heal; a time to break down, and a time to build up;
>
> A time to weep, and a time to laugh; a time to mourn and a time to dance. . . .
>
> It is better to go to the house of mourning, than to go to the house of feasting; for that *is* the end of all men; and the living will lay *it* to his heart.
>
> Sorrow is better than laughter; for by the sadness of the countenance the heart is made better.
>
> The heart of the wise *is* in the house of mourning; but the heart of fools *is* in the house of mirth.[28]

Strange as it may seem, the individual in being lonely, if let be, will realize himself in loneliness and create a bond or sense of fundamental relatedness with others. Loneliness rather than separating the individual or causing a break or division of self, expands the individual's wholeness, perceptiveness, sensitivity, and humanity. It enables the person to realize human ties and awarenesses hitherto unknown. In loneliness one is definitely alone, cut off from human companionship.

Being lonely calls for a taxing and straining of resources which toughens the individual for facing the realities of life. Most individuals today would rather not be faced with an experience which is so all-encompassing of self, which calls for the full use of human potentialities, which calls for such deep intense feeling. And most of us would rather not stand by while another plunges into such a totally desolate existence. Therefore, every effort is made to provide the lonely one with company, to get him involved in a social life, to keep him busy with obligations and tasks. It is too disturbing to let the solitary person be, to remain with him while he lives through a pitiful or tragic situation. So we escape our own discomfort and pain, and contribute to the unrealized loneliness of the other person by surrounding him with company, by talking him out of his deep depression, by getting him into other experiences as quickly as possible, by assigning him tasks which will get his mind off his plight.

The experience of seeing another person in lonely suffering is so piercingly effective, that we use every means to terminate the situation, providing new conditions and requiring a prescribed set of acts or behavior.

---

[28] London and Foreign Bible Society, *op. cit.*

48   CONCEPTS OF LONELINESS

Alone sometimes has a positive meaning. There is more recognition today of individuality and the dangers of conformity. We are more apt to think twice before interrupting an individual when he is alone in thought or meditation or when he plunges into a solitary endeavor. But loneliness is almost always regarded as destructive and the common social urge is to rescue the lonely one. This social urge is often motivated by an inability to bear or tolerate suffering.

There is no solution to loneliness but to accept it, face it, live with it, and let it be. All it requires is the right to emerge in genuine form.

In the spiritual and creative experience, there is often no other way but the lonely way, perceiving life from one's own being, creating oneself as one wants to be, drawing upon one's own resources, capacities, roots—searching, suffering, struggling to emerge from one's own inner solitude, in a quiet place. In such experiences, there is often a fixed determination to go one's own way and a courage to stand alone. The creative person is often lonely because he must be a world in himself and must find the way in life within himself.

Oliver Wendell Holmes expressed this conviction in his address before Harvard University students in 1886.

> To think great thought you must be heroes as well as idealists. Only when you have worked alone—when you have felt around you a black gulf of solitude more isolating than that which surrounds the dying man, and in hope and in despair have trusted to your own unshaken will—then only will you have achieved. Thus only can you gain the secret isolated joy of the thinker, who knows that a hundred years after he is dead and forgotten men who never heard of him will be moving to the measure of his thought—the subtle rapture of a postponed power, which the world knows not because it has no external trappings, but which to his prophetic vision is more real than that which commands an army.[29]

Chesterton, in his essay on loneliness, was convinced that the work of English poets and novelists emerged in most original and unique form and grew best when their lives were quiet and detached. He emphatically believed in loneliness as a basic value in life, proclaiming:

> And I do seriously think that Englishmen ought to make some fight for that right of ancient sanctuary, before it is broken down by the mere American herd-instinct. I have never been a Jingo, or uttered political boasts

---

[29] Oliver Wendell Holmes, "The Profession of the Law," *Speeches* (Boston: Little, Brown & Company, 1913), p. 22. Reprinted by permission of the Law School of Harvard University.

about the Splendid Isolation of England, but I would do a great deal to preserve the Splendid Isolation of Englishmen.[30]

He emphasized the absolute need to take an active stand in defense of loneliness because he was finding it increasingly difficult to take a lonely walk or find a lonely path, or spend a lonely evening. Thoreau spent many years alone in the woods. In *Walden* he wrote:

I have never felt lonesome, or at least oppressed by a sense of solitude, but once, and that was a few weeks after I came to the woods, when, for an hour, I doubted if the near neighborhood of man was not essential to a serene and healthy life. To be alone was something unpleasant.[31]

He soon realized that the fancied advantages of human neighborhood were insignificant.

What do we want most to dwell near to? Not to many men, surely, the depot, the post office, the bar-room, the meeting-house, the grocery, Beacon Hill, or the Five Points, where men most congregate, but to the perennial source of our life, whence in all our experience we have found that to issue, as the willow stands near the water and sends out its roots in that direction. This will vary with different natures, but this is the place where a wise man will dig his cellar.[32]

Thoreau discovered that loneliness held a positive meaning and value which enabled him to experience a fundamental continuity with nature. One day in the midst of a gentle rain he became suddenly aware of

such sweet and beneficent society in nature, in the very pattering of the drops, and in every sound and sight . . . an infinite and unaccountable friendliness all at once like an atmosphere sustaining me. . . . Every little pine needle expanded and swelled with sympathy and befriended me.[33]

The loneliness of his life was not unbearable, not thwarting or limiting at all, not foreign. On the contrary, he felt it wholesome to be alone a great part of the time. He loved to be alone and never found loneliness wearisome or dissipating. He "never found the companion that was so companionable as solitude."

I am no more lonely than a single mullein or dandelion in a pasture, or a bean leaf, or sorrel, or a horsefly, or a bumblebee. I am no more lonely

[30] G. K. Chesterton, *Come To Think Of It* (New York: Dodd, Mead & Co., 1931), p. 98. Reprinted by permission of Miss D. E. Collins.
[31] Henry David Thoreau, *Walden and Other Writings*, Brooks Atkinson, ed., Modern Library (New York: Random House, Inc., 1937), p. 119.
[32] *Ibid.*, p. 121.
[33] *Ibid.*, p. 119.

than the Mill Brook, or a weathercock, or the North Star, or the south wind, or an April shower, or a January thaw, or the first spider in a new house.[34]

Loneliness is a condition of existence which leads to deeper perception, greater awareness and sensitivity, and insights into one's own being. New images, symbols, and ideas spring from the lonely path. The man living his life, accepting all significant dimensions of human existence is often a tragic man but he is a man who loves life dearly. And out of the pain or loss, the bitter ecstasy of brief knowing and having, comes the glory of a single moment and the creation of a song for joy.[35] In creative loneliness there is an element of separation, of being utterly alone, but there is also a strange kind of relatedness—to nature and to other persons and through these experiences, a relatedness to life itself, to inspiration, wisdom, beauty, simplicity, value. A sense of isolation and solitude is experienced, but a relatedness to the universe is maintained. Only through fundamental relatedness can the individual develop his own identity. The individual's loneliness is an experience in growing which leads to differentiation of self. The person's identity comes into relief as he breathes his own spirit into everything he touches, as he relates significantly and openly with others and with the universe.

Without any deep and growing roots in the soil of loneliness, the individual moves in accordance with external signals. He does not know his place in the world, his position, where he is or who he is. He has lost touch with his own nature, his own spontaneity.

To the degree that the individual strives to attain a similarity or congruity, to the degree that he acts in order to be popular, to be victorious or to be approved of, he fails to emerge as a self, fails to develop his unique identity, fails to grow as a creative being consistent with his own desires and capacities and consistent with a life of genuine relatedness to others.

In actualizing one's self, one's aspirations, ideals, and interests, it is often necessary to retreat from the world. One must have strength enough to withstand the temptations which arise when one is completely alone. This does not mean becoming uprooted or alienated. It means accepting the existential nature of man's loneliness and seeing its value in the creation of being, in the emergence of self-identity, and in a more fundamental, genuine life. Cast in this light, loneliness becomes an illuminating experience and it leads to greater heights.

[34] *Ibid.*, p. 124.
[35] Wolfe, *op. cit.*, p. 66.

A beautiful image of the significance of the lonely experience is created by Gibran in the following poem.

Defeat, my Defeat, my solitude and my aloofness:
    You are dearer to me than a thousand triumphs,
    And sweeter to my heart than all world-glory.

Defeat, my Defeat, my self-knowledge and my defiance,
    Through you I know that I am yet young and swift of foot
And not to be trapped by withering laurels.
    And in you I have found aloneness
And the joy of being shunned and scorned.

Defeat, my Defeat, my shining sword and shield,
    In your eyes I have read
That to be enthroned is to be enslaved,
    And to be understood is to be levelled down,
And to be grasped is but to reach one's fulness
    And like a ripe fruit to fall and be consumed.

Defeat, my Defeat, my bold companion,
    You shall hear my songs and my cries and my silences,
And none but you shall speak to me of the beating of wings,
    And urging of seas,
And of mountains that burn in the night,
    And you alone shall climb my steep and rocky soul.

Defeat, my Defeat, my deathless courage,
    You and I shall laugh together with the storm,
And together we shall dig graves for all that die in us,
    And we shall stand in the sun with a will,
And we shall be dangerous.[36]

The deep experiences in life can often be shared only in silence and communal loneliness. In moments of great grief, suffering, pain, loss, one can only stand by sharing the horror and misery, participating in still companionship, letting the loneliness be, letting it unfold into various realms of human emotions, various nuances of feelings and awarenesses. In the times when the sense of loneliness is most piercing and unbearable we can relate to others who feel and share the same loneliness and isolation, and we can relate to nature. Such depth of loneliness cannot be understood or communicated but it can be shared, as in the case of this young man who conveyed his deep experience of loneliness in the following letter written after part of his art exhibit was ravished and stolen.

[36] Kahlil Gibran, *The Madman* (New York: Alfred A. Knopf, Inc., 1918), pp. 46-48.
Reprinted by permission of the publisher.

The air wonders at the snow's begin. I feel I best wonder where snow ends. The intense feelings of sorrow yesterday, the night beginning at dusk when I tried to sleep, the night of disbelief at what people will do. The bronze sculpture gone, the black painting torn. My pot broken, sand spilled, the terrible chattering room—The death of my life. At first I could not utter a sound, then it was hopeless to do so. Just a pot. Just a sculpture. Just a painting. Just a life and a life—my life. They say build another pot, make another sculpture, but they do not realize that life in each has its distinct essence never to be in another form. Where does the spirit of such life go? Why are people so cruel and thoughtless of life? I can build, and will new life but I am so painfully ashamed at the awareness of people. Art should never be locked or guarded from the lives of people. Why can they not be as noble as the breath given them? What is art to be guarded, locked, policed, untouched? Why can man not realize that his life and that of all life are the same and that each has its identity only in the ability to share essences? This incident is a haunting reminder of the weak morality of our *well* society. They feed on the waste of their own existences and think it alive and beautiful.

I learned pain this day. I learned pain. We never own our lives or anything. Our possession is *nothing*. Naked of want, nothing remains! We do not really create anything. We are but the means to present another individual entity without claim to its life. At any time the pot can be broken. Broken! Broken! Broken! The trees make no lament, yet they know the same awaits them. And we also know. Why are men so insensitive to beauty? I cannot stand their coarse screams and the murder of whatever God means in Beauty. Where is nowhere where one can be at peace?

This experience has taught me much pain. We can not be so foolish as to be possessors of life. We can not be so vain as to say "ours." We do not create anything by cognitive wish only by the love felt of the material but then we must guard against the desire to hold. How hard it is to be content with the empty left by something we love that has gone.

Someone must have had a great need to possess my sculpture to have taken it. But gladly would I have given it to anyone who would have loved it. This does not trouble me nearly so much as the death of my pot. To be a destroyer of life is immorality, severe in even the world of the bean. . . . The life of these words to you are perhaps my new beginning.

The swallow always wins, even now I feel better and maybe I will be able to work again. I hope so. To meet the matter death with calm is the only way, perhaps, to life.

Many times I have found courage and strength and beauty through loneliness, in an experience with nature.[37] One day I was feeling deeply depressed by the severe criticisms a colleague had received—a person who was living his life in an honest and truthful sense, attempting to express

[37] Clark E. Moustakas, "Creativity, Conformity, and the Self," *Creativity and Psychological Health*, Michael Andrews, ed. (Syracuse, N.Y.: Syracuse University Press, in press). Reprinted by permission of the editor.

his unique nature in his work. I felt especially saddened when I realized how he had suffered, when all he wanted to do was maintain a personal and creative identity, a genuine existence and relatedness. I felt especially sensitive to pretense and surface behavior. Nothing was real. It disturbed me to see each situation as contrived, as feigned. Yet I could not call forth my own being even where there was a possibility for a genuine meeting. A numbness had settled in, right at the center of my thought and feeling. That night even the children were unable to shake my grief and sadness. In their own spontaneous, unknowing ways, they tugged and pulled at me to draw me into life, but for me there remained only suffering in the world.

After the children had gone to bed, I decided to go for a walk. The night was dark, filled with black clouds. Large white flakes of snow fell on and around me. Inside, a surging restlessness replaced my benumbed state. The night was silent and serene in spite of the atmospheric turbulence. Suddenly, without understanding in any way, I experienced a transcendental beauty in the white darkness. It was difficult to walk on the glazed, iced surface but as I walked I felt drawn to the black, inky streaks embedded in the treacherous ice. Dark wavy lines spread out in grotesque forms which were partly covered by snow. I knelt down, touching the black, irregular patterns and letting them enter inside me. Immediately I felt a chill but at the same time I felt the ice being warmed as my fingers touched it. It was a moment of communion, an experience of knowing and understanding, and a feeling of complete solace. I felt my inward heaviness lifting, and discovered a new capacity for exertion and endurance, for openly and directly facing conflicts which existed around and in me. I realized how, out of broken roots and fibers, how out of deep loneliness, a genuine encounter may occur and make possible the discovery of a new level of individual identity and new strength and conviction. I realized how the self can be shattered in surface and false meetings when surrounded by extensive pressures to conform, and how in communion with nature the self can reach a new dimension of optimism and a new recognition of the creative way of life. Possibilities for unique and unusual meetings exist everywhere. We need only reach out in natural covering to come face to face with creation.

IV

THE ISOLATED MAN

Every man is alone. Ultimately, each person exists in isolation. He faces himself in silence, wending his way in individual pathways, seeking companionship, reaching out to others. Forever, man moves forward stretching to the skies, searching the realization of his own capacities. In loneliness, man seeks the fulfillment of his inner nature. He maps new meanings, and perceives new patterns for old ways and habits. Alone, the life of man passes before him. His philosophy, the meanings he attaches to his work and his relations, each significant aspect of his being comes into view as new values are formed, as man resolves to bring human significance, to bring life to each new day, to each piece of work, to each creation.

In loneliness, every experience is alive and vivid and full of meaning. When one has been greatly isolated and restricted in movement, one deeply feels the value of openness, of freedom and expansiveness. Life takes on an exquisite meaning, an exhilarating richness. When one has lived in total darkness, one piercingly appreciates the sunlight, the fireside, the beacon, the beginning dawn. When one is cut off from human companionship, one discovers a deep reverence for friendship, for the one who stands by in the hour of need and shame. In the days of pain and defeat, loneliness takes on a human depth. When one is sequestered from life, when one is purely alone and dying, when one is lost in a world of dreary emptiness then color becomes exquisite, rich, desirable, fulfilling. When one has been sharply isolated and lonely, every moment is pure, every sound is delightful, every aspect of the universe takes on a value and meaning, an exquisite beauty. The isolated tree stretches out to meet its new neighbor; the lonely star twinkles and turns to face its emerging companions in the night; the lost child runs to loved ones with open arms.

Each of us has been alone and lonely, starved for companionship. Each of us has endured days or weeks of isolation. Then suddenly, miraculously, we greet each face with a radiance and warmth, with a spirit of kinship, with a deeper and more genuine fellowship, in a totally different way than when we are constantly in the presence of others.

Every lonely man experiences deep joy and gladness, rapture and awe in the presence of a human voice, the variations of musical tone, of volume and pitch, the miracle of silent eyes, the quiet touch of a human hand, the ecstasy of simply standing face to face, or walking shoulder to shoulder with one's fellow man. Each man comes to recognize the richness of the blue sky, the white clouds, the brilliant colors of the rainbow, the glorious opening of a new flower, each item is born anew and takes on an entirely unique value. The lonely mountain climber, the isolated explorer, the pilot lost in the desert, the sailor adrift at sea—each has known the agony and despair of loneliness. Each has discovered within horrible starvation, disease, and unbearable freezing the growing terror of an untimely death. Each of us has searched within for a new meaning in life, a value in being alive, in breathing freely, in walking openly, in conversing with companions. In the face of final death, in isolation and loneliness, the discovery is made that life is rich in its resources and its ways, that truth is universal, that wisdom and love and reverence are rooted in every living meeting, that each individual stretches forward to touch a universal humanity.

In time of abiding loneliness and suffering the value and meaning of life are re-examined. Men lost in the mountains, in the desert, at sea, men faced with slow, painful death, men craving food and water, begin to consider the past. They search for deeper meanings in life. They review their relations. They hear again the words of love and hate they have spoken, the individuals they have violated with criticisms, recriminations, and competitive victories. They relive the scenes of meanness, pettiness, and dishonesty. They feel again the attachments they have known, the tender and cooperative endeavors. Everything of import comes to mind. The isolated man searches for answers to life. He seeks a better life. He wishes to be reconciled to himself and others. He realizes the necessity of turning to lofty ideals, of finding the good and the beautiful in life, the simple and the true. In these hours he is honest and direct in facing his conflicts and problems, and in questioning his values. He searches for a genuine basis for living, a way of loving every human being, a way to life in which each man is respected and valued, in which each man is encouraged to find himself and his own quantum in life. The lost and lonely man seeks deliverance. He seeks to be forgiven his trespasses. He yearns for one more chance to absolve himself and his misdeeds, to rectify his sins against his fellow man, to turn the misery he has created into joy and happiness. In the face of slow death, each man in his own way turns to God.

This self-searching, this recognition of evil and striving for good, this search for truth and wisdom and beauty and love, was the experience of each man in the crew transporting Captain Rickenbacker on an official mission to islands in the Pacific during World War II. The plane crashed and the men were lost twenty-one days at sea. In the beginning many were atheists or agnostics, but at the end of this terrible ordeal each man, in his own way, discovered God. Each man found God in the vast, empty loneliness of the ocean. From the worn Bible of Sgt. Bartek, each man found salvation and strength in prayer.[1] From two strange miracles which the men felt saved their lives, a new faith emerged and a community of feeling developed which created a liveliness of human fellowship and worship, and a sense of gentle peace. Two of the prayers which bound the group together, and provided hope and communion in the hours of great fear and utter loneliness follow. I present these prayers because they enabled frightened men to find truth and wisdom and beauty and love and strength in hours of terrifying loneliness.

1.

O Lord, rebuke me not in thy wrath: neither chasten me in thy hot displeasure. For thine arrows stick fast in me, and thy hand presseth me sore. There is no soundness in my flesh because of thine anger; neither is there any rest in my bones because of my sin. For mine iniquities are gone over mine head; as an heavy burden they are too heavy for me. My wounds stink and are corrupt because of my foolishness. I am troubled; I am bowed down greatly; I go mourning all the day long. For my loins are filled with a loathsome disease; and there is no soundness in my flesh. I am feeble and sore broken: I have roared by reason of the disquietness of my heart. Lord, all my desire is before thee; and my groaning is not hid from thee. My heart panteth, my strength faileth me; as for the light of mine eyes, it also is gone from me. My lovers and my friends stand aloof from my sore; and my kinsmen stand afar off. They also that seek after my life lay snares for me; and they that seek my hurt speak mischievous things, and imagine deceits all the day long. But I, as a deaf

[1] Johnny Bartek, *Life Out There* (New York: Charles Scribner's Sons, 1943).

man, heard not; and I was as a dumb man that openeth not his mouth. Thus I was as a man that heareth not, and in whose mouth are no reproofs. For in thee, O Lord, do I hope: thou wilt hear, O Lord my God. For I said, Hear me, lest otherwise they should rejoice over me: when my feet slippeth, they magnify themselves against me. For I am ready to halt, and my sorrow is continually before me. For I will declare mine iniquity; I will be sorry for my sin. But mine enemies are lively, and they are strong: and they that hate me wrongfully are multiplied. They also that render evil for good are mine adversaries; because I follow the thing that good is. Forsake me not, O Lord: O my God, be not far from me. Make haste to help me, O Lord my salvation.

2.

Judge not, that ye be not judged. For with what judgment ye judge, ye shall be judged: and with what measure ye mete, it shall be measured to you again. And why beholdest thou the mote that is in thy brother's eye, but considerest not the beam that is in thine own eye? Or how wilt thou say to thy brother, Let me pull out the mote out of thine eye; and, behold, a beam is in thine own eye? Thou hypocrite, first cast out the beam out of thine own eye; and then shalt thou see clearly to cast out the mote out of thy brother's eye. Give not that which is holy unto the dogs, neither cast ye your pearls before swine, lest they trample them under their feet, and turn again and rend you. Ask, and it shall be given you; seek, and ye shall find; knock, and it shall be opened unto you: For every one that asketh receiveth; and he that seeketh findeth; and to him that knocketh it shall be opened. Or what man is there of you, whom if his son ask bread, will he give him a stone? Or if he ask a fish, will he give him a serpent? If ye then, being evil, know how to give good gifts unto your children, how much more shall your Father which is in heaven give good things to them that ask him? Therefore all things whatsoever ye would that ye should do to you, do ye even so to them: for this is the law and the prophets. Enter ye in at the strait gate: for wide is the gate, and broad is the way, that leadeth to destruction, and many there be which go in thereat; Because strait is the gate, and narrow is the way, which leadeth unto life, and few there be that find it. Beware of false prophets, which come to you in sheeps' clothing, but inwardly they are ravening wolves. Ye shall know them by their fruits. Do men gather grapes of thornes, or figs of thistles? Even so every good tree bringeth forth good fruit; but a corrupt tree bringeth forth evil fruit. A good tree cannot bring forth evil fruit, neither can a corrupt tree bring forth good fruit. Every tree that bringeth not forth good fruit is hewn down and cast into the fire. Wherefore by their fruits ye shall know them. Not every one that saith unto me, Lord, Lord, shall enter into the kingdom of heaven; but he that doeth the will of my Father which is in heaven. Many will say to me in that day, Lord, Lord, have we not prophesied in thy name? and in thy name have cast out devils? and in thy name done many wonderful works? And then will I profess unto them, I never knew you: depart from me, ye that work iniquity. Therefore whosoever heareth these sayings of mine, and doeth them, I will liken him unto a wise man, which built his house upon a rock: and the rain descended, and the floods came, and the winds blew, and beat upon that house: and it fell not: for it was founded upon a rock. And every one that heareth these sayings of mine, and doeth them not, shall be likened unto a foolish man, which built his house upon the sand: And the rain descended, and the floods came, and the winds blew, and beat upon that house; and it fell: and great was the fall of it. And it came to pass, when Jesus had ended these sayings, the people were astonished at his doctrine: For he taught them as one having authority, and not as the scribes.

Antoine de Saint-Exupéry

In the pioneering days of aviation, men were frequently lost at sea, in the mountains, in the desert. Many died alone—of hunger, thirst, freezing temperatures, at the hands of hostile tribes—when they survived the crashing. The lonely pilot came to know the precious nature of life, the absolute necessity of making each moment a living one, making every encounter a significant meeting, bringing each potential creation to fulfillment. He soon realized a sense of isolation and solitude, the deep loss when his companion did not return. A malady grew within him as he waited for his friend to return. And in his heart each moment of waiting was eternity, each vision of horror endless. Until finally he knew his comrade would not come back, that he had joined, in ultimate slumber, the rocks of the mountains, the sands of the desert, the waters of the sea, the stars and wind of the night.

The hours of silence and loneliness cultivate a deepened sense of values in life. The brevity of life becomes a startling reality. Time is short and man must find his place in the universe. Man must leave the traces of his life in nature and in the depths of human hearts and minds. Man must reach others vitally and fundamentally and share in a communion which gives each being a sense of honor and a sense of knowing and belonging.

Life is brief. Alone, man recognizes in his heart the wonder and awe of human life. The whole world grows old. What remains must be left to be. Flowers bloom, radiantly, brilliantly, even in the frost. The grain ripens in the field even in the night. Trees bring forth their leaves and fruit even in the cold. Life is passing. Man must savor each living experience and shine forth as a unique human being, as unique as a bright flare on a distant horizon in a silent night.

Saint-Exupéry describes the ultimate loneliness of separation and death as follows:

> Bit by bit, nevertheless, it comes over us that we shall never again hear the laughter of our friend, that this one garden is forever locked against us. And at that moment begins our true mourning, which, though it may not be rending, is yet a little bitter. For nothing, in truth, can replace that companion. Old friends cannot be created out of hand. Nothing can match the treasure of common memories, of trials endured together, of quarrels and reconciliations and generous emotions. It is idle, having planted an acorn in the morning, to expect that afternoon to sit in the shade of the oak.[2]

Lost in the desert, in danger, naked between sand and sky, withdrawn from life by enduring silence, Saint-Exupéry realized the full meaning of loneliness. He knew if he were not sighted he would die of thirst or starvation, or be found and murdered by the Moors. Yet in the days of aloneness in the desert he discovered himself and a life filled with dreams. Only when he felt the last moments approaching did he see that he must remain truly alive, vital, awake to the very end, moving forwards, with arms outstretched for those who would be waiting and searching for him. He came out of the desert with his heart and mind alive. He found himself, in what appeared to be the beginning of the end, in the presence of a truth which he had failed to recognize. He reached rock-bottom loneliness and despair. Yet, instead of sinking into a state of self-estrangement, he experienced a strange, exulting, gentle peace. Later, he saw that in such an hour man finds himself and becomes his own friend. He does not feel sorrow or cry out in grief but he possesses a kind of wealth—the awareness of the unity of existence, of man's relatedness to all of life. He finds he is the desert and the desert is him.

Saint-Exupéry came to understand himself and the nature of man in days and nights in the sand, although the awareness of these realities often did not strike home until a later time. He knew that in loneliness an essential inner need is satisfied and that no external power can ever prevail against self-fulfillment.

> Never shall I forget that, lying buried to the chin in sand, strangled slowly to death by thirst, my heart was infinitely warm beneath the desert stars.
> What can men do to make known to themselves this sense of deliverance? Everything about mankind is paradox. He who strives and conquers grows

[2] Antoine de Saint-Exupéry, *Wind, Sand and Stars*, Lewis Galantiere, trans. (New York: Reynal & Hitchcock, 1939), pp. 44-45. Copyright © 1939 by Antoine de Saint-Exupéry; reprinted by permission of Harcourt, Brace & World, Inc.

soft. The magnanimous man grown rich becomes mean. The creative artist for whom everything is made easy nods. Every doctrine swears that it can breed men, but none can tell us in advance what sort it will breed. . . . Of what can we be certain except this—that we are fertilized by mysterious circumstances? Where is man's truth to be found?

Truth is not that which can be demonstrated by the aid of logic. If orange-trees are hardy and rich in fruit in this bit of soil and not that, then this bit of soil is what is truth for orange trees. If a particular religion, or culture, or scale of values, if one form of activity rather than another, brings self-fulfillment to a man, releases the prince asleep within him unknown to himself, then that scale of values, that culture, that form of activity, constitute his truth.[3]

These insights sometimes came suddenly in lonely hours, in isolation. Sometimes they emerged gradually, naturally, in the midst of living. Saint-Exupéry let himself be, and in being and waiting he realized the treasure of the human voice, the beauty of the smile, the wonder and glowing fulfillment of human companionship. He knew that man waxes and blooms in the presence of his comrades, that the joys of human relations are as vast as the ocean, that only in the warmth of human life can man find true happiness. And in the lonely hours he knew the meaning of freedom. He knew his life had relevance, his work had purpose.

What all of us want is to be set free. The man who sinks his pickaxe into the ground wants that stroke to mean something. The convict's stroke is not the same as the prospector's, for the obvious reason that the prospector's stroke has meaning and the convict's stroke has none. It would be a mistake to think that the prison exists at the point where the convict's stroke is dealt. Prison is not a mere physical horror. It is using a pickaxe to no purpose that makes a prison; the horror resides in the failure to enlist all those who swing the pick in the community of mankind.[4]

In loneliness, in the dark hours, Saint-Exupéry did not die. He came to feel an aliveness he had never known before. He came to feel an awareness of life, of man and nature, a vividness and clarity of purpose as resounding as chimes of the church extoling a universal birth, ringing the call to humanity, mirroring the joy of a resurrection. He came to see that all men wish to come alive, that many are imprisoned by self-estrangement, by extraneous values and standards, by a mechanical and machine-like existence. Man strives to break bread with his fellow man, to share the heart-breaks and joys of life, to awaken in the presence of the human touch. All of us express at bottom the same exalted impulse to

[3] *Ibid.*, pp. 240-241.
[4] *Ibid.*, p. 292.

meet our comrades on a meaningful, living basis. In the hours that truly count, man lives with other human beings in richness which cannot be bought. Saint-Exupéry deeply felt the priceless nature of human relations.

> One cannot buy the friendship . . . of a companion to whom one is bound forever by ordeals suffered in common. There is no buying the night flight with its hundred thousand stars, its serenity, its few hours of sovereignty. It is not money that can procure for us that new vision of the world won through hardship—those trees, flowers, women, those treasures made fresh by the dew and color of life which the dawn restores to us, this concert of little things that sustain us and constitute our compensation.[5]

Simple ideas, so obvious, yet so rarely seen, so rarely entering into modern life.

For Saint-Exupéry, being separate and alone, brought deepening awareness and growing wisdom into basic human values. He brought with him a rapturous commitment to his fellow man and within this commitment he discovered the foundation for compassion, self-fulfillment, and living happiness.

HERMANN BUHL

When Hermann Buhl reached the highest peak in the Himalayas, he did not feel any great joy and enthusiasm or any great thrill of accomplishment even though he was the first man to reach the summit. He had suffered great pain and had faced almost certain death. There was no moving exhilaration. He was alone, overcome with waves of shattering desolation. He had been cut-off from his expedition, warned by his leaders not to continue the climb upward to Nanga Parbat, the peak above 26,000 feet. But he went on—alone—in spite of the fact that he was warned, severely admonished, even ordered by his leaders to return to the Base Camp. There was no support, no affirmation from his group. He was on his own now in a journey to the summit. He was soon to experience horrors he had never known—avalanches, spraying his face and body with wet. heavy snow, freezing his boots, clogging his rubbers with rime as he climbed upward. He was to know terrible searing thirst, his tongue glued to his gums, his throat raw as a rasp. He was to experience

[5] Ibid., pp. 45-46.

the torture of murderous heat, a veritable agony of hell, driving him literally mad, causing dehydration, making his blood thick and viscous. His yearning for drinkable liquid—a single drop of tea—was deep, endless. He was to experience the most terrible fear and loneliness he had ever known, falling down, utterly exhausted, crawling, losing balance, taking each step upward and downward with almost complete immobility and loss of control. After every step his weary body sank down into the snow. But somehow when all his strength seemed gone, an inner spark emerged to keep him going. He was barely able to get up, to stand, to move on. But there was no other way to get back to living people and the desire for human companionship was as great as the need for liquid and food. He had to stand all night in total darkness on a meager platform, which barely provided room for both his feet —much too small to sit down. He could hardly stay upright. His head fell forward; his eyelids pressed like lead. He dozed off. He tried to keep awake but sleep kept defeating him—miraculously he did not lose his balance. He would wake with a start, realizing his isolation, knowing he was on a steep rock slope high up on Nanga Parbat, exposed to cold and darkness, with a black silent abyss waiting below. He found he had to yield continually under stress until he reached the end of his resources, until there was nothing left to yield with.

During the hours of extreme tension and loneliness, he had a "partner" with him, looking after him, taking care of him, belaying him. He was to hear voices calling his name, calling again and again. He wanted to shout, to cheer, to be recognized but he could not produce a sound. And when he struggled, fought nearly insurmountable obstacles, to go out to meet "them" there was no one there, nothing but a vast expanse of empty space. He knew he was definitely alone, isolated in a hopeless, endless waste of ice above 26,000 feet. And he was to feel many times he had reached the end of life. Yet in these terrifying, lonely hours, he discovered the precious nature of life, the sheer beauty of being alive. He knew the full meaning of having climbed the mountain and understood the simple truth that he climbed solely because the mountain existed. It was there to climb. His was a simple desire to see and feel and touch and experience the reality of the mountain peak and the lonely challenge it created. His whole life took on a new meaning in that lonely waste of ice. He resolved if he came out alive to devote himself to good and creative works. He realized as never before the richness and miracle of human companionship. In the struggle, on his way to reaching the top, he found a few genuine friends in his expedition—not the leaders, not the great climbers, but simple men who had gone as far as they could with him and wished him well in the final journey. He wrote on his return:

> They never even asked whether I had gotten to the top; all that seemed to matter was that I was back safely. Our close communion at that moment was for me the most significant experience of the whole expedition, for we had established something more than the camaraderie of team-mates—a true and deep friendship.[6]

In his loneliness, Buhl discovered the wonder and joy of life. He realized the absolute requirement of love and human companionship in deriving meaning and purpose in life. And he knew within himself that every reality in nature and humanity existed to be known in genuine experience.

ADMIRAL RICHARD E. BYRD

Admiral Byrd spent nearly six months alone on an advanced base in Antarctica. He wanted to gather meteorological data which would provide valuable information on Antarctica. But he also desired to be alone, to be by himself, to savor the peace and quiet and solitude of loneliness long enough to find out if he really believed in himself, if his values in life held genuine significance and enduring meaning. Beset by the complexities of modern life, he wished desperately for some silent place to re-examine his way of life and to search into his thoughts, to reason undisturbed, to some natural conclusion. He asked himself, "Must you go off and bury yourself in the middle of polar cold and darkness just to be alone? After all, a stranger walking down Fifth Avenue can be just as lonely as a traveler wandering in the desert." Yet Byrd was a famous explorer. His commitments and fame prevented him from being alone long enough to discover what truly mattered in life. So he chose a life of self-isolation.

Alone in Antarctica, each sound took on a distinct and special meaning. Each experience held a vital significance. In temperatures which ranged to −74°F, if there were the slightest breeze, he could hear his breath freeze as it floated away and it made a tremendous sound like

[6] Hermann Buhl, *Lonely Challenge*, Hugh Merrick, trans. (New York: E. P. Dutton & Co., Inc., 1956), p. 292. Reprinted by permission of the publisher.

the explosion of a firecracker. There were sounds which were crushing, isolating. Byrd wrote:

> There is something extravagantly insensate about an Antarctic blizzard at night. Its vindictiveness cannot be measured on an anemometer sheet. It is more than just wind: it is a solid wall of snow moving at gale force, pounding like surf. The whole malevolent rush is concentrated upon you as upon a personal enemy. In the senseless explosion of sound you are reduced to a crawling thing on the margin of a disintegrating world; you can't see, you can't hear, you can hardly move. The lungs gasp after the air sucked out of them, and the brain is shaken. Nothing in the world will so quickly isolate a man.[7]

In lonely hours, Byrd could realize a new meaning; he could discover the precious nature of each living thing. He could experience the harmony and unity of man and nature, the universal oneness of all beings, the relatedness of night and day, of man and the cosmos. He observed in the darkening twilight:

> The day was dying, the night being born—but with great peace. Here were the imponderable processes and forces of the cosmos, harmonious and soundless. Harmony, that was it! That was what came out of the silence— a gentle rhythm, the strain of a perfect chord, the music of the spheres, perhaps.
>
> It was enough to catch that rhythm, momentarily to be myself a part of it. In that instant I could feel no doubt of man's oneness with the universe. The conviction came that that rhythm was too orderly, too harmonious, too perfect to be a product of blind chance—that, therefore, there must be purpose in the whole and that man was part of that whole and not an accidental offshoot. It was a feeling that transcended reason; that went to the heart of man's despair and found it groundless. The universe was a cosmos, not a chaos; man was as rightfully a part of that cosmos as were the day and night.[8]

Byrd soon discovered the brain-cracking loneliness of solitary confinement and the loneliness of futile routine. He tried to crowd his days with systematic but meaningful acts. But he found it exceedingly difficult to escape loneliness. He could not take it casually. It was too big, too compelling. Each new day opened and closed in darkness. The cold and darkness depleted his body and eroded his mind. He had to admit he was lonely. But only after much struggle to overcome his loneliness and to avoid dwelling on it, did he realize its significance. He tried to

[7] Richard E. Byrd, *Alone* (New York: G. P. Putnam's Sons, 1938), pp. 154-155. Copyright © 1938 by Richard E. Byrd; reprinted by permission of the publishers.
[8] *Ibid.*, p. 85.

focus his mind, his thinking, only on healthy constructive images and concepts because he was frightened by lonely thoughts.

In spite of sheer concentration and every effort of will power, Byrd could not avoid the terrible evenness and loneliness of silence. For the quiet was as real and solid as sound, as awakening as the creaks of the ice barrier and the concussions of heavy snow, as relentless as the ticking of a clock.

Byrd anticipated the crisis of loneliness. What he had not counted on was how closely a man could come to dying and still not die or want to die. He suffered indescribable pain and terror, being poisoned by carbon monoxide, not believing he had the strength to live through months of severe illness, unaided and alone. Yet he kept going even when all his powers and resources seemed completely exhuasted, even when he experienced excruciating fear and pain, as globules of ice clung to his eyelashes, freezing them together, blinding him until they melted, as his fingers froze, as the skin came off his face and hands as he touched metal surfaces. During his hours of bitter loneliness, when he became utterly aware and sensible, he understood the ultimate meaning of being alone. He realized how wrong his sense of values had been and how he had failed to see that the simple, the natural, the homely, the unpretentious things in life are what really matter.

Being alone, experiencing deep, raw loneliness helped Byrd find new meanings in old patterns, helped him evolve a humble set of values. He discovered the obvious—the simple beauty of every living creation in the universe—but he had to live through cataclysmic loneliness, and a totally debilitating illness to see and hear, and feel, and touch, and know the sheer beauty and miracle of being alive and being related.

NED LANGFORD

From ancient history to the present, the individual afflicted with leprosy has always been regarded as loathesome. The horror and revulsion of such a person is so great he is inevitably treated as a pariah. The disease so repels most people they prefer to keep entirely away from the leper, not wishing to come even within speaking distance. In the presence of leprosy, we forget that the afflicted person is a human being. We feel deep aversion and often become offensive in our rejection of him. He is made to feel that he is the invidious germ itself spewing out in all directions. His mental anguish is far more terrible than any physical discomfort. No one is more immediately isolated and cut-off from normal human intercourse, more totally rejected socially. It is easy to see from the brutal rejection why the individual suffering from Hansen's disease can view himself as some inhuman creature crawling out from under a rock. No criminal condemned to solitary confinement is confronted with such torture and loneliness. The terribly painful, silently endured loneliness of the leper is impossible to comprehend except by those having faced the dreadful disease.

Something of the analogy to a pestilent, disgusting animal was the perception of Ned Langford when he knew with certainty, for the first time, that the growing, unfeeling spots on his body were the first stages of leprosy. The physician making the diagnosis took him to a dilapidated shack, in a place that was completely sequestered. Adjacent to the shack was the city dump. Ned Langford immediately realized the significance of this hideout, and as immediately he regarded himself as part of the refuse. His dull, gloomy state of mind made him feel as worthless as the heap of useless rubbish which surrounded him. At that moment, he knew he was lost to humanity. His life was totally devoid of any value. He was now to be shunned by society; totally left out. He belonged with all the other worthless leavings in the world.

But he did not immediately realize that he would have to fight for his place—even in a dump. As he opened the door of the broken-down shack, droves of large rats scurried through it. Terrified, he entered and quickly bolted the door. A sickening, savage battle resulted for prior claim. Perry Burgess tells the story for Ned, in the following passages.

There was one left, a huge devil of a rodent in the far corner, disputing possession with me. I started to the door to unfasten it, when, without warning, he flew at me, hit my leg with terrific force, his teeth ripping through my trousers. I lurched back, but I caught him with my foot and kicked, sending him against the opposite wall. He squealed shrilly and flew at me a second time. I snatched up the only chair and hurled it, and the thing went to pieces. He had turned and was on me again. This time he leaped high and I struck at him with my clenched fist and he clung to my coat. He dropped to the floor. I kicked at him but missed; he was too quick for me. I stopped to pick up the chair leg and like lightning he was on my hand, tearing, tearing! I grabbed frantically and found his throat. He let out one bloodcurdling squeal as my hands closed on him. He fought and clawed, cutting my hands until the blood streamed. I was afraid to let go. He was limp, he must be dead, but I hung on. Then I swung my arms and hurled him, dead, through the glass in the window.

With the sound of breaking glass something crashed within me. Alone, alone for all time: Mother! Mabel! Tom! Jane! Jane . . . Jane . . . for the first time in my memory I began to sob. I reeled across to the wooden bunk, threw myself down, and wept my heart out.[9]

This was only the beginning of Ned's painful terror and the deadening isolation he was to feel. The impact of his dangerous infection seeped through his body, turning his veins to ice and shriveling his heart. He would never again see his family, his fiancée, his friends. He would never again enter his home, his town, which held his belongings and his treasures. He would never again know the world of his childhood and his youth. Now he would have to go through the motions of a meaningless existence.

For the next year his life was a hideous nightmare. He buried himself in an obscure shack in New York City while submitting to secretive medical treatment, as an experiment in arresting the disease. There were nearly five million people who shared the same spaces but he was not permitted to speak or be near any of them. He was to remain always alone. He avoided the subway, the trolley, the trains—any place where other human beings congregated. Many nights he could not sleep. He roamed the streets, keeping his distance from the laughing voices, merriment, and gala celebrations, from the bright lights and brilliant colors. His heart was filled with despair and sadness and his mind shook with thoughts of self-defeat and physical destruction. He walked and walked, away from people, alone. He thought and suffered to the point of extreme isolation and self-contempt. He wrote his brother Tom:

> You could never believe how alone loneliness is. You have to move, live, breathe, see, hear, in the midst of millions of people, not daring to touch one of them, afraid to speak lest they become friendly—avoiding—avoiding—eternally avoiding.
>
> There were times when he wanted to protest against his self-enforced isolation. He wanted to scream, "Look, everyone! Look at me! My name is Ned Langford and I'm a man, too. I'm a human just as much as you are." [10]

Yet Ned never attacked or condemned anyone or shouted for his rights when society did violence to him as a human being, and caused him drastically to deteriorate in his sense of dignity and integrity. He never blamed others for the hours he spent avoiding people, for the terror he knew at being singled out, for the pain he experienced in feeling accusingly fingered as a leper. There were times when he wanted to end his

---

[9] Perry Burgess, *Who Walk Alone* (New York: Holt, Rinehart and Winston, Inc., 1940), p. 44. Reprinted by permission of the publishers.
[10] *Ibid.*, p. 70.

misery and loneliness through self-inflicted death, when he yearned for permanent peaceful slumber, but each time he thought of suicide he remembered his brother's words, "Don't ever just quit"; and he kept on fighting. Once in a great while he felt human and whole again, such as when his physician put an arm around his shoulder. This act moved him so deeply that his self-repulsion melted. He was momentarily warmed by the thought that the doctor cared enough to touch him spontaneously, lovingly, as a natural way to assuage that fitful terror in his heart.

After his year in New York, Ned decided he could not continue hiding, escaping from the world. He knew he would have to join others afflicted with leprosy; he would have to have human companionship to want to live. So he chose San Lazaro in the Philippines as his "sanctuary of sorrow." His utter despair continued for a long time. His loneliness, his refusal to accept the disease as final, his unwillingness to believe that he would never again know his life in America, that he would never again be with his family, filled him with agony. The horror of it all struck him to the depth of his soul when he found his Filipino friend dying. The decaying body before him frightened him beyond description as he saw the eyebrows and eyelashes gone, the forehead covered with shiny, reddish welts, some of which were open wounds. The bridge of the nose had fallen in; the nostrils were swollen with festering tubercules. The lips were thick and enlarged. His friend tried to speak but his voice was queer and weak and hoarse. The strange sounds were incoherent, meaningless. Ned felt he was being addressed by a dead person. This final painful meeting left him with an indelible image even though he learned that most lepers do not deteriorate so completely.

Hope surged within him when he came to live with other lepers, when he submitted to the medical program. He kept alive a dream of recovery for many, many years—finding salvation and joy in work and in nature, and finding surpassing value in a lonely life. The dream lived on within him. Even when the disease began to spread, he plunged more deeply into creating and nourishing the flowers and grasses and trees surrounding his home, which had been bequeathed to him by a former leper who died in San Lazaro. But in the end the dream was broken. He was forced to surrender. On November 11, as the First World War terminated, he too signed an armistice with Hansen's disease. He knew he would never recover. He accepted with final resignation the fact that he would never return home cured. On this momentous occasion, he signed his name as a symbol of submitting. Thus he abandoned his right to mingle with Americans without fear and without shame. At the same time he realized there was something very special in his life as a leper over the twenty-

five years. There was something of rare significance in his years of loneliness when he was almost completely isolated from his own people. This
life was special in a way he had not expected, in a way he had
never known. For all the lonely suffering, he never had to pretend to
be other than he was. He could always speak directly, honestly, without
sham, without ulterior motive, without any objective beyond meeting
the other person in a simple, open way. He said what he wanted to say
and thought what he wanted to think. As a leper he had a striking in-
dependence different from anything he had known as a "normal" man.
He had a community of neighbors who were open with him, who knew
and respected him as a genuine person. And he had his home, his own
place, partly created with his own hands, a home he had achieved
through sheer exercising of his talents and capacities, a home achieved
against sickness, against loneliness, against despair, against so many terrors and breakings of the heart and mind. For twenty-five years on a
little island, Ned lived as a lonely person never reaching the full depths
of human companionship but knowing the tender love and communion
of fellow sufferers and joy and fulfillment through work. What did it all
mean? Nearing the end, he understood the meaning of life. He came to
know that no matter how life is lived it is always strange, always a mystery
—that one must live with whatever comes—not being defeated or overwhelmed, but searching for glory in pain, finding victory in defeat, knowing relatedness in loneliness, and emerging with strength and fortitude
from experiences of isolation and suffering. At last he saw that one must
meet life with courage, without complaint, as it is, or be crushed and dis-
owned by it.

Without warning, it came to Ned one night, with a full tide of feeling. He wanted to go to the home of his childhood. He wanted to touch
American soil again. He was sick and old and tired. He yearned once more
for the land of his youth and early manhood. He wanted to see the sun
rising over the plains, the cattle grazing on the hillsides, the maples
growing in the grove beyond the farmhouses, the fields, the roads, the
sky, the fertile valley, the smoke from the factories, the red-brick stores.
He wanted to see his countrymen; once again to be in the land he loved.
In his final words, he spoke with joy and optimism.

> . . . at the end of twenty-five years in a leper colony, this leper knows
> that he is, first of all, a man. For that man life has been worth while. . . .
> In the flesh I am still in prison. But the essential "I" has escaped. I am
> free. My spirit is out in the fields, in the woods, running through the
> towns. I am living my youth, the youth that followed the flag to the
> Orient nearly forty years ago. All the years of suffering, of horror, of

hope and despair, fade into oblivion. Tomorrow this train, and I in it, will pass through the very town where I was born! [11]

In his dying hours, Ned passed through his town. Briefly, he knew and held all the savoring visions of his early life in America. He had attained a growing individuality through a life of disease, through years of isolation and loneliness. He had grown a life which he himself came to regard and value as worth while.

EMILY DICKINSON

Emily Dickinson lived alone, in almost complete isolation, for a quarter of a century, the last years of her life. Privately, she loved a man for almost twenty years whom she had seen face to face no more than three or four times and who was unaware of the depth and intensity of her devotion. Much of her poetry was inspired by this intimate, monastic attachment. Its force continued to give direction to her productive capabilities for the rest of her life.

She was a rare, unusual, gifted person who could not find a place for herself in society, and whose only salvation was a lonely, solitary existence. She often stood out as the lone dissenter in her youth when she made efforts to meet others on an honest basis. She stated her convictions even when they removed her from the appropriate and acceptable modes of behavior and from the proper groups.

While attending Mount Holyoke Female Seminary she searched to find the existence of God but she emerged with less than absolute devotion. Her non-Christian ways created much consternation among her family, teachers, and classmates. She could not readily accept the standards of Christian living imposed by the college, nor the precepts and prayers for redemption. She lived a life of hardship as a non-believer in an institution founded and dedicated to Puritan rigor and religious worship. She was one of the few who did not rise when Miss Lyon, the Principal, wished to see the faces of all who had been saved. Rollo Brown wrote of her individuality, as follows.

> The most heroic display of courage in New England was not at Concord Bridge or Bunker Hill, but in Mount Holyoke Female Seminary. Principal Mary Lyon had just made her announcement to the young ladies assembled in chapel that Christmas was to be celebrated as a fast. After she had awed—or bullied—the hesitant into acceptance, she asked—that is, dared— any dissenter to rise. And Emily Dickinson stood up.

[11] *Ibid.*, pp. 294-297.

Merely to be the solitary dissenter required courage enough. Unsympathetic eyes on every side, supported by stout authority, have driven many a college girl to surrender convictions that she had believed were laws of nature—and possibly were. Unsympathetic eyes on every side, without the official support, have caused many another to turn away from college brokenhearted. Emily Dickinson did not choose to surrender. Nor did she decide to go home—except for a rebellious celebration of Christmas. Instead, in a little world where it was proper to think as the majority thought, and where the majority had much of its thinking done by somebody else, she dared to express the sense of fitness cherished by the minority.[12]

Emily Dickinson remained spiritually intransigent to the end of her seminary experience. Even when she felt grave danger that one of her very few ties would be severed if she did not declare a Christian faith, she could not revise her ways, writing:

Sue—you can go or stay—There is but one alternative—We differ often lately, and this must be the last.

You need not fear to leave me lest I should be alone, for I often part with things I fancy I have loved—sometimes to the grave, and sometimes to an oblivion rather bitterer than death—thus my heart bleeds so frequently that I shan't mind the hemorrhage, and I only add an agony to several previous ones, and at the end of day remark—a bubble burst!

Such incidents would grieve me when I was but a child, and perhaps I could have wept when little feet hard by mine, stood still in the coffin, but eyes grow dry sometimes, and hearts get crisp and cinder, and has as lief burn. Sue—I have lived by this. It is the lingering emblem of the Heaven I once dreamed, and though if this is taken, I shall remain alone, and though in that last day, the Jesus Christ you love, remark he does not know me—there is a darker spirit will not disown it's child.

Few have been given me—and if I love them so, that for *idolatry*, they are removed from me—I simply murmur *gone*, and the billow dies away into the boundless blue, and no one knows but me, that one went down today. We have walked very pleasantly—Perhaps this is the point at which our paths diverge—then pass on singing Sue, and up the distant hill I journey on.[13]

Emily Dickinson did not give up the world but neither could she find herself in the world, so she retired from it. Only by violating a purity of self, only by denying her inspirations, and values and purposes, only by distorting her private perceptions and experiences could she achieve

[12] Rollo Walter Brown, *Lonely Americans* (New York: Coward-McCann, Inc., 1929), pp. 235-236.

[13] Thomas H. Johnson and Theodora V. W. Ward, eds., *The Letters of Emily Dickinson*, Vol. I (Cambridge, Mass.: The Belknap Press of Harvard University Press, 1958), pp. 305-306. Copyright © 1958 by The President and Fellows of Harvard College; reprinted by permission of the publishers.

an acceptable place and be approved by others. Only by compromising, by distorting, by abstracting from her total experience what could be confirmed, by using a common language, by employing recognizable standards and forms could she have lived in society. She had to resist being warped into something resentful and ugly by a practical society, by the values of a middle-class education and culture, and by the evangelical demands of her community. She resisted by choosing a life of seclusion as the only way of life by which she could consolidate her resources and express her talents in unique, poetic forms. The loneliness and simplicity of her life enabled her to live in accordance with her private experiences and convictions and to realize her talents. Her indifference to professional or artistic goals and to social recognition, she expresses in the following poem.

> How happy is the little Stone
> That rambles in the Road alone,
> And doesn't care about Careers
> And Exigencies never fears-
> Whose Coat of elemental Brown
> A passing Universe put on,
> And independent as the Sun
> Associates or glows alone,
> Fulfilling absolute Decree
> In casual simplicity.[14]

Through a reclusive life she maintained her health and her sanity. She enjoyed a gentle peacefulness and serenity. Through loneliness, she preserved her integrity, her individuality. In this, she remained private, immovable, proud. She achieved a victory, living creatively in isolation, never being forced to bitterness, retaliation, hatred, but always maintaining a pure identity of love, gentleness, and understanding combined with wisdom, determination, and a powerful authenticity.

When the man she idolized moved to a distant state and her lonely heart was breaking, when his removal seemed a permanent living entombment, she portrayed the depth of loneliness and separation, the catastrophic yet beautiful experience, exclaiming:

> I know that he exists, somewhere in silence
> I envy seas whereon he rides
> I tend flowers for thee, bright absentee
> At least to pray is left, is left

[14] Thomas H. Johnson, ed., *The Poems of Emily Dickinson*, Vol. III (Cambridge, Mass.: The Belknap Press of Harvard University Press, 1955), p. 1042. Copyright © 1951, 1955 by The President and Fellows of Harvard College; reprinted by permission of the publishers.

> Is bliss then such abyss
> After great pain a formal feeling comes
> It will be summer eventually
> 'Twas the old road through pain[15]

Her poetry was her way of maintaining an inner life and growing in isolation and loneliness. In these poetic forms Emily Dickinson lives forever, bringing gladness and joy, depth of feeling and understanding, to thousands of human hearts. Her poems were conceived in lonely hours. They depict the incongruity of man and the universe, the loneliness man feels in separating himself from the universe, the tragedy of man's self-estrangement and alienation from nature. Her poems empowered her to endure life and attain a fortitude and intuitive vision into the unknowable, into nature, beauty, the ordinary experiences of life, and into death and immortality.

The sense of cosmic loneliness in which nature participates in the loneliness felt by man is expressed with a deep perceptiveness in the following poem.

> Further in Summer than the Birds
> Pathetic from the Grass
> A minor Nation celebrates
> It's unobtrusive Mass.
>
> No Ordinance is seen
> So gradual the Grace
> A pensive Custom it becomes
> Enlarging Loneliness.
>
> Antiquest felt at Noon
> When August burning low
> Calls forth his spectral canticle
> Repose to typify
>
> Remit as yet no Grace
> No Furrow on the Glow
> Yet a Druidic Difference
> Enhances Nature now[16]

In the winter of 1871 she wrote, "The terror of the winter has made a little creature of me, who thought myself so bold." In 1874, her father, for whom she held a peculiar but deep devotion, was seriously ill. He suffered from a disquieting inner loneliness much of his life. The sight of his lonesome face was more terrible to Emily Dickinson than any per-

---

[15] *Ibid.*, Vol. I, p. 270. Copyright © 1951, 1955 by The President and Fellows of Harvard College; reprinted by permission of the publishers.

[16] *Ibid.*, Vol. II, p. 752. Copyright © 1951, 1955 by The President and Fellows of Harvard College; reprinted by permission of the publishers.

sonal or social strife. She wrote, "I think his physical life don't want to live any longer. You know he never played, and the straightest engine has its leaning hour." [17] Edward Dickinson led a lonely life and he died a lonely death.

Her "death" poems bring the person immediately in touch, so close to the experience of death, so startlingly real, that one can feel its imminence and nature, as in the following poems.

> Yet able to contain
> A Rudiment of Paradise
> In it's diminished Plane.

> A Grave - is a restricted Breadth -
> Yet ampler than the Sun-
> And all the Seas He populates
> And Lands He looks upon

> To Him who on it's small Repose
> Bestows a single Friend
> Circumference without Relief-
> Or Estimate - or End -[18]

>   .   .   .

> And then I heard them lift a Box
> And creak across my Soul
> With those same Boots of Lead, again,
> Then Space - began to toll,

> As All the Heavens were a Bell,
> And Being, but an Ear,
> And I, and Silence, some strange Race
> Wrecked, solitary, here -

> And then a Plank in Reason, broke,
> And I dropped down, and down -
> And hit a World, at every plunge,
> And Finished knowing - then -[19]

Richard Chase describes Miss Dickinson's victory, as follows.

Her antagonist was nothing less than society itself, and the public opinion through which the values of society were forced upon the individual. She was entirely content to be what the world called a "nobody" so long as her position as "nobody" could be used as a vantage point. . . . And in her way she defeated the world, finally overwhelming its most

[17] Quoted in Richard Chase, *Emily Dickinson* (New York: William Sloane Associates, 1951), p. 257. Copyright © 1951; reprinted by permission of the publishers.
[18] Johnson, *op. cit.*, Vol. II, p. 685. Copyright © 1951, 1955 by The President and Fellows of Harvard College; reprinted by permission of the publishers.
[19] *Ibid.*, Vol. I, pp. 199-200. Copyright © 1951, 1955 by The President and Fellows of Harvard College; reprinted by permission of the publishers.

stubbornly held redoubts. Her strategy was elaborate and extreme; it involved her own death. Emily Dickinson's seclusion—sad as it was and unpropitious for our culture—was yet one of the notable acts of our history.[20]

In one way or another, most of Emily Dickinson's poems bear irrevocably the depth of her isolation and loneliness. But it was a way of life she chose because she felt she must. She gave to her seclusion a range of significance beyond herself. She gave it a liveliness and beauty, an experiential quality that enabled her to commune with many frightened lonely souls, unaware of their own separation from life.

[20] Chase, *op cit.*, pp. 268-269.

V

The Loneliness of Public Life

The President

Every position of great responsibility entails searching hours of lone-liness. When decisions which have far-reaching consequences for others must be made, the person in the executive chair must stand alone and often suffer in silence from inevitable criticism and hostility. Nearly every step the official takes will be lauded by some and condemned by others. Perhaps no position is more exacting and more isolating than that of President of the United States. The president is constantly surrounded by people and incessantly faced with pressures and demands. He sees many people every day who wish to influence him in some way, but rarely does he enter into genuine and fundamental relationships. The one pri-mary element in life—human depth in love for its own value—is often missing. The president is frequently subjected to malicious gossip, slan-der, and backbiting. Nearly every word he speaks, each and every act of his behavior, is made newsworthy and publicized. Forever, there is some individual or group which evaluates and maligns him, more often as a result of hindsight than foresight. And there are almost as many second-guessers as there are voters. The presidency is a position of vast scope re-quiring the making of decisions based on experiences and data which no one person can fully absorb.

In the preface of his memoirs, Harry S. Truman wrote:

> Very few are ever authorized to speak for the President. No one can make decisions for him. No one can know all the processes of his thinking in making important decisions. Even those closest to him, even members of

his immediate family, never know all the reasons why he does certain things and why he comes to certain conclusions. To be President of the United States is to be lonely, very lonely at times of great decisions. . . . The pressures and the complexities of the presidency have grown to a state where they are almost too much for one man to endure. Important decisions cannot wait. A President must decide not only on the facts but the experience and preparation he brings to them. It is a terrible handicap for a new President to step into office and be confronted with a whole series of critical decisions without adequate briefing.[1]

No time is more isolating, more soul-searching for the president, than a time of war when each major decision he makes may result in the extermination of thousands of human beings. During war, as Commander-in-Chief, the president assumes new, far-reaching responsibilities; the whole future of human freedom is at stake. Inevitably, waging a war is an unpopular cause.

The isolation of command is deeply felt when there is no one with whom the responsibilities of the presidency may be shared, when there is no one with whom the president may talk openly and freely without fear of being misunderstood or without departing from the ethics of office. As a rule, the president is hesitant to admit his doubts, fears, ignorance, or conflicts because of the threat of violating the confidentiality of his office or of losing face or prestige. There is often no way to vital human companionship in the crucial issues. From the ultimate burden of decision there is no relief; his is a loneliness of command.

Abraham Lincoln

Nearly all his life Abraham Lincoln found himself alone. In his childhood, he walked, and thought, and read on his own—striving to find a meaningful place and bring a sense of enrichment to his life. He knew many hours of solitude, many hours of deep melancholy, and many hours of mental exertion in long-continued thought. He was frequently restless and gloomy and desperate. As a young man, he was denied fulfillment in his relationship with the one lady he truly loved. When Ann Rutledge died he was terribly grieved, so much so that his power of reason was endangered. He wandered aimlessly—alone—feeling entirely estranged from the world and not caring whether he lived or died. His depression and despair were so great that he came close to mental derangement. He often appeared on the brink of suicide. His first and perhaps

[1] Harry S. Truman, *Memoirs: Years of Trial and Hope*, Vol. II (New York: Doubleday & Co., 1956). Copyright © 1956 by Time Inc.; reprinted by permission of the editors of *Life*.

only great love was rudely torn from him and all the world seemed empty and gray and cold. His affliction was almost beyond endurance. He never felt the world as a place of joy. He was convinced he was doomed from the first to a melancholy existence. The one characteristic which remained fixed was his sad, pained facial expression. He was usually awkward with others and deeply sensitive to his clumsiness.

After his initial defection at the wedding with Mary Todd, he said:

> I am now the most miserable man living. If what I feel were equally distributed to the whole human family, there would not be one cheerful face on earth. Whether I shall ever be better, I cannot tell; I awfully forbode I shall not. To remain as I am is impossible. I must die or be better, as it appears to me.[2]

Eventually he married Mary Todd—though he never loved her and after his failure to appear at the first wedding she never loved him. In her wrath, she was bent on avenging his abasement of her. In contemplating marriage with her, he was faced a second time with a great conflict: to keep his pledge, thereby maintaining his honor, or to continue to search for domestic peace. He chose to keep his word and because of it suffered years of self-inflicted torture and sacrifice and the loss of a happy home life forever.

His life with Mary Todd was filled with painful issues and demands in which he was constantly attacked, criticized, and belittled. At times in his law office, his distress was so plain and his silence so significant that his law-partner, William Herndon, unable to bear the loneliness and pain, was forced to leave the room.

Long before he became president, Lincoln contended he was destined for a terrible fate. He frequently repeated his certainty that he would come to some terrible end. Two things intensified his characteristic loneliness: one was the endless succession of trouble in his domestic life which he had to bear in silence and the other was his awareness of his own obscure and lowly origin.

Once in handling a divorce case in which the husband enumerated instances of marital suffering, Lincoln interrupted him and said, "My friend, I regret to hear this; but let me ask you in all candor, can't you endure for a few moments what I have had as my daily portion for the last fifteen years?" [3] He spoke so mournfully and with such a look of distress the husband was completely disarmed.

When he was laboring under a dejection of spirit there was a song

---

[2] William Herndon and Jesse W. Weik, *Abraham Lincoln* (New York: D. Appleton & Co., 1920), p. 201. Reprinted by permission of Appleton-Century-Crofts, Inc.
[3] *Ibid.*, p. 140.

which struck a responsive chord in his heart. This song, which follows, reflects the sorrow, gloom, and loneliness of his life. It reflects his search for joy and happiness and freedom of spirit and his conviction that such soaring human elevation comes only with death.

Tell me, ye winged winds
That round my pathway roar,
Do ye not know some spot
Where mortals weep no more?
Some lone and pleasant vale
Some valley in the West,
Where, free from toil and pain,
The weary soul may rest?
The loud wind dwindled to a whisper low,
And sighed for pity as it answered, No.

Tell me, thou mighty deep,
Whose billows round me play,
Know'st thou some favored spot,
Some island far away,
Where weary man may find
The bliss for which he sighs:
Where sorrow never lives
And friendship never dies?
The loud waves rolling in perpetual flow
Stopped for a while and sighed to answer, No.

And Thou, serenest moon,
That with such holy face
Dost look upon the Earth
Asleep in Night's embrace—
Tell me, in all thy round
Hast thou not seen some spot
Where miserable man
Might find a happier lot?
Behind a cloud the moon withdrew in woe
And a voice sweet but sad responded, No.

Tell me, my secret soul,
Oh, tell me, Hope and Faith,
Is there no resting-place
From sorrow, sin, and death?
Is there no happy spot
Where mortals may be blessed,
Where grief may find a balm
And weariness a rest?
Faith, Hope, and Love, best boon to mortals given,
Waved their bright wings and whispered, Yes, in Heaven.[4]

[4] A poem written by Charles Mackay, a British writer who was war correspondent for a London newspaper in the Unitel States during the Rebellion.

His loneliness in life strengthened Lincoln, enabled him to develop a depth of awareness and sensitivity. It made possible his deepness of thought and feeling for humanity. It enabled him to realize the significance of genuine meetings in human life. It helped him to see the value of truth and candor, and of sincerity in his relations. It enabled him to listen to every person with utter respect and to listen with reverence. Through his solitude he developed a gentleness of spirit and a kindliness toward all men. When it came to justice and right and liberty no man could ever move him. He was as adamant and unrelenting as gravity itself. He held firm in his lofty ideals for humanity. He knew from his own lonely existence the meaning and significance of the good in contrast to evil, the value of love and justice and freedom in human life. He never refused to see people and was deeply sensitive to human suffering and misery, putting all his powers to work to effect a better life for those who lived in pain.

Lincoln was a controversial figure from the very beginning of his political career. He frequently was defeated in his attempts to secure public office. He was not willing to accept compromise but held to an exact position on the great social questions of his time. The hostility against him was extreme. Many threats on his life were made when he was about to be inaugurated as president. He was warned that he would never pass through Baltimore alive on his way to Washington—making it necessary for General Scott to provide military protection.

Rumors were rampant that once Lincoln had achieved the highest public office, he cared no more for his home or friends, that he was ashamed of his earlier affiliations and associations, that he did not remember any of the people who had assisted him to the presidency. Office-seekers pursued him relentlessly, dogging his steps wherever he went, edging their way through crowds and thrusting their papers in his hands, slipping through half-opened doors to the executive mansion, using every strategy and device to receive special favors and nearly worrying him to death. His life became so pressured and burdened that he moved about in an abstracted, mechanical way, seemingly cut-off from himself and unaware of the humanity for which he gave his life. His sadness and despair grew through the war years as he felt the tragedy of death and the destructiveness of war. His melancholy was expressed in every breath he took; it literally saturated every word he spoke, every step he took. It was ingrained, so deeply impressed that he could only rarely feel joy, gladness, concrete relatedness to man or nature.

He seldom depended on others; he was a man true to his own lights, relying on his own searching solitude for insights. He thought alone. His forte lay in digging out for himself and securing for his mind its own food, to be assimilated unto itself. He had a great power for seeing into the heart of an issue, for absorbing the raw elements, and reasoning in a pure way divested of all distortion and delusion.

Lincoln loved humanity but in an abstract way. He did not know the concrete love of individuals as it grew and deepened from the heart. His was a general love of human beings everywhere rather than a love for his neighbors. It is sad to relate that he was never aware of the deep and abiding love which human beings everywhere felt for him. Perhaps Americans themselves did not realize how deeply they revered him until after his death. He was a great man and he lived a life of deep sadness and loneliness. His love for humanity will live in the heart of man forever. America today can still feel the tragedy of his assassination. The decisions he made as president continue to affect man's destiny and man's strivings for a better world.

We can understand and appreciate the indescribable shock of his fellow countrymen when news reached them of Lincoln's death. William Herndon expresses the wave of anguish which spread everywhere in these passages:

> In every household throughout the length and bredth of the land there was a dull and bitter agony as the telegraph bore tidings of the awful deed. The public heart, filled with joy over the news of Appomattox, now sank low with a sacred terror as the sad tidings from the Capitol came in. In the great cities of the land all business instantly ceased. Flags drooped half-mast from every winged messenger of the sea, from every church spire, and from every public building. Thousands upon thousands, drawn by a common feeling, crowded around every place of public resort and listened eagerly to whatever any public speaker chose to say. Men met in the streets and pressed each other's hands in silence, and burst into tears. The whole nation, which the previous day had been jubilant and hopeful, was precipitated into the depths of a profound and tender woe. It was a memorable spectacle to the world—a whole nation plunged into heartfelt grief and the deepest sorrow.[5]

Only after Lincoln had fallen, leaving "a lonesome place against the sky" was his true magnitude realized.[6] Only then was the loftiness of his soul recognized in all its aloneness.

---

[5] Herndon and Weik, *op. cit.*, pp. 279-280. Reprinted by permission of Appleton-Century-Crofts, Inc.
[6] Brown, *op. cit.*

Woodrow Wilson

Woodrow Wilson had a dream for world peace, a vision to which he could dedicate himself in a total sense. He worked feverishly to bring about friendship, love, harmony, unity in the world. After he had convinced other major nations of the absolute necessity of a world peace organization, after he had pursed his vision with tireless effort, after he had strained and stretched every physical resource and mental ability, after he finally achieved a significant victory in foreign lands, he was defeated by political jealousies and machinations in his own country.

Woodrow Wilson believed that to live in harmony the world required two simple but inclusive principles—the right of self-determination of peoples of every nation in the world and a world association for mutual aid and protection and for the elimination of war. Both of these central concepts—American in origin—were vanquished on American soil. Ralph McGill describes the ruination of Wilson in the following passages.

> At whatever cost, Lodge and Baker, with their personal grievances, their partisan passion, felt Wilson must be destroyed. The way to destroy him was to discredit and defeat the great project which he had brought to the verge of success. Their own words of former days would come back to belie them, but they were too angry and desperate to care for that. It was a titanic task, but Lodge was a master at manipulating the forces which could be worked to confuse the people and defeat their desires.[7]

Wilson's great efforts to bring a lasting peace to a war-weary world lost out to partisan politics and bitter personal feelings of retaliation. His defeat was a triumph for the isolationists. It was the final blow to a man who had struggled all his life to show his inner disposition and humaneness, a man who felt deep sympathy in his relations with others, but who was inevitably kept away as an icy, machine-like person. Woodrow Wilson experienced frequent feelings of isolation and restraint in his relations with others. He wanted people to recognize him as a warm, feeling person. He wanted people to understand and love him but he believed they never would—and for the most part, he was not loved as a humanitarian until some time after his death.

> Sometimes I am a bit ashamed of myself when I think how few friends I have amidst a host of acquaintances. Plenty of people offer me their

---

friendship; but, partly because I am reserved and shy, and partly because I am fastidious and have a narrow, uncatholic taste in friends, I reject the offer in almost every case; and then am dismayed to look about and see how few persons in the world stand near and know me as I am—in such wise that they can give me sympathy and close support of heart. Perhaps it is because when I give at all I want to give my whole heart, and I feel that so few want it all, or would return measure for measure.[8]

He often felt even his own individuality, his own freedom blotted out, eradicated in the terrible burdens of public life. He was beseeched at every turn by callers galore who sought to influence his thinking or gain his support. He was expected to attend innumerable public ceremonies. He had to participate in endless meetings. As president, he was never able to be himself, never able to meet people on a fundamental basis. He described a typical Sunday as a day in which he sat at the edge of his front porch flanked by a row of militia officers, gazed at without relief, while a chaplain conducted services on his lawn, with a full brass band to play the tunes for the hymns; followed by lunch in his home for the chaplains, Catholic priests, and anyone else who happened along. In the afternoon he received and paid military calls and attended reviews. In the evening callers from all over the country beckoned at his door. He had no time for his own thoughts, no time to be alone, to be free with his own loneliness, no time to call up his own stirrings of the heart and mind, to experience the sweet richness of a life that emerges in its own time and way. He had no private life at all. The office of president brought him no personal blessing, only "irreparable loss and desperate suffering." He yearned to disguise himself and be a free man and have a joyous time again. To a personal friend, he wrote:

It's an awful thing to be President of the United States. It means giving up nearly everything that one holds dear. When a man enters the White House, he might as well say, "all hope abandon, ye who enter here." The presidency becomes a barrier between a man and his wife, between a man and his children. He is no longer his own master—he is a slave to the job. He may indulge no longer in the luxury of free action or even free speech.[9]

As president, he could not express all that he thought. His opinions could not be uttered freely and spontaneously. They had to be toned down and filtered to a respectable and solemn level.

There were always rumors, malicious gossip, and name calling. Theo-

[8] Donald Day, ed., *Woodrow Wilson's Own Story* (Boston: Little, Brown & Company, 1952), p. 67. Reprinted by permission of the publishers.
[9] *Ibid.*, p. 118.

dore Roosevelt called him a "Byzantine legothete" (a man who expounds
but never acts) and a "damned hypocrite." He was frequently de-
nounced as lacking moral and intellectual fibre. He was maligned with
words to tear him down, "Egotist," "Coward," "Faker," "hogging the
whole show." A torrent of verbal missiles followed him wherever he
went, aimed at destroying his reputation and his honor. He expressed the
fear of being overwhelmed and crushed by the constant maledictions
against him. He exclaimed in a solitary moment in a quiet place:

> the world grows sometimes to seem so brutal, so naked of beauty, so devoid
> of chivalrous sentiment and all sense of fair play, that one's own spirit
> hardens and is in danger of losing its fineness.[10]

Mr. Wilson sadly proclaimed that he had never read an article in which
he recognized himself. He sometimes wondered whether he was some
kind of fraud because of the consistent discrepancy between his own perceptions and the views of others who wrote and spoke about him. He
spent many lonely hours trying to understand how he could create so
many varied and false impressions.

When his first wife died, while he was in office, his isolation and loneliness increased terribly and became widespread. Even this suffering
could not be done nobly, alone, peacefully. There were slanderous
rumors that he had carried on affairs with other women, that his marriage
had been empty of love and hope and beauty, that his home had been
filled with icy meetings and discordant situations. Later, when he married
Ellen Bolling, rumors spread that she "bought off" the "other women."
Yet she alone could assuage his increasing, intolerable suffering during
the terrible years of war, when he sought passionately to find a formula
which would end the slaughter. Only intimate associates were aware of
his growing anguish and knew the pain of his restless soul. Bowers
observes how Wilson's excruciating distress at the declaration of war was
rarely recognized by the public:

> He suffered from the slings and arrows of his enemies, but he did not
> reveal his wounds in public, since he was proud. . . . His secretary has
> given us one picture that throws a vivid light on his character. The editor
> of a paper of the opposition had written him a letter that was kindly and
> sympathetic just before our declaration of war. "That man understood me
> and sympathized," he said as he drew his handkerchief and wiped tears
> from his eyes. Then laying his head on the table he sobbed. He faced his

[10] *Ibid.*, p. 132.

enemies with cold pride but a kindly word revealed the heart of the man, a lonely man, facing the necessity of sending American boys to war.[11]

Wilson hated and dreaded war. He suffered continual agony throughout the war and ached over every terrible death and maiming.

He sought in vain for some respite from the relentless pressures and the tragedies which faced him every day. He played golf, went to the theater, plunged into various activities which might amuse him— but the deadening weight was always there. "Even then," he wrote, "it is lonely, very lonely. And it is then that I have *time* to miss my friends and consciously wish for them." He searched inwardly to find some answer to his grief and loneliness, to bring meaning and new life to his responsibilities as president, but he became increasingly isolated, separated from his own spontaneous and tender nature, from his own fun-loving, prankish ways.

Woodrow Wilson loved his fellow countrymen with a deep and genuine compassion. He gave his life for central values and convictions which he came to only after much internal struggle, deliberation, and lonely self-reflection. His dream was for all humanity everywhere; but he was regarded with suspicion and seen as a heartless intellectual. In the end, he fell a victim in spite of his courage and valor. Only a few realized that humanity had suffered a tragic loss. Now we know that his vision was a humanic enterprise born out of a hatred for evil, destruction and war, grown from a desire for peace and harmony and freedom. Only now are we certain that his dream must become an enduring reality or humanity faces extinction. In his time he lived in isolation, but today Woodrow Wilson is cherished and loved, for he provided a way to a friendly life among nations. He crusaded and died for a plan for world peace with which his name will be identified forever.

THE PERSON WHO STANDS ALONE

The person who expresses strong convictions in everyday life inevitably stands alone. He experiences many hours of loneliness because he adheres to his own values and refuses to compromise. The lone dissenter often must withdraw from the world; his deviation is threatening and

[11] Claude J. Bowers, "The Statesman," *The Greatness of Woodrow Wilson*, Em Bowles Alsop, ed. (New York: Holt, Rinehart and Winston, Inc., 1956), pp. 165-166. Reprinted by permission of the publishers.

disturbing to others. His ideas and thoughts require others to examine their own inner conscience and responsibility. Such a challenge provokes conflict and arouses fear and insecurity in others.

The individual who stands alone is often reviled when he acts contrary to public opinion or when he threatens the security of his nation. The poet, the statesman, the president, the person in public life who is disgraced, all are individuals who have suffered from a sense of being alienated from society, a sense of being misjudged, misinterpreted, and dispossessed. All are individuals who have been exposed to the loneliness of public condemnation and rejection. All are individuals who have submitted to the loneliness of fame or infamy and to the loneliness of public responsibility or private confinement. All are individuals isolated from society, yet they often maintain an unyielding integrity and strength.

Benedict Arnold

Benedict Arnold was one of the most lonely, and perhaps most hated, persons in American history. Many Americans since the days of the revolution have united to curse his memory, to execrate him, and to keep his infamy alive. In 1780, one of his former "friends" wrote, "Even villains less guilty than himself will not cease to upbraid him and tho' they 'approve the treason they will despise the traitor!' "

All his life, from his early childhood to his untimely, poverty-stricken death, Benedict Arnold sought respect and status. He strove for acceptance and recognition from the aristocratic families, the cultured and educated groups, the leaders of the American Revolution and the Congress. He was never actually held in esteem by any of these groups. His one stirring ambition was to achieve social rank. In this he was constantly checked and stifled. His unceasing effort to be valued by the status and power groups ended in failure. He suffered frequent rebuffs from the Congress and frequent character assaults by his enemies. He was deprived again and again in battle of a clear and shining victory because of the competitive strivings for power of American officers who were above him in command and to whom Arnold consistently refused to subordinate himself. Although he was recognized as an outstanding field commander with flaming personal courage, in one way or another his brilliance in battle was marred either by other generals or unfortunate circumstances.

His success at Fort Ticonderoga was contested by Ethan Allen. The continual deceit and bickering between them as to who was the real hero and who was in charge, coupled with the political intrigue within the

Congress, left Arnold with a feeling of uncertain achievement. The crushing blow to Arnold at Ticonderoga was delivered by the state of Massachusetts, which cast aspersions on his character and insultingly placed him under the command of a lesser figure. He was frustrated again and again in his attempt to conquer Quebec. He had marched from the Maine wilderness to Quebec, enduring sickness, terrible disease, starvation, and cold, finally besieging the city during the worst winter in a generation. Many of his men deserted or left as their enlistment period ended; an entire division returned to Massachusetts. Through the treachery of his own advance messengers the British had been warned, and during inspection, Arnold discovered that a large part of the rifles, muskets, and cartridges were defective. At last he realized there would be no surpassing honor in Quebec. The assault failed, Arnold was wounded in action, and withdrawal from Canada was the only course left. Even for the great victories at Saratoga in which he figured prominently, he did not receive the accolade for splendid triumph.

If ever there was a maligned and maltreated officer of the army it was Arnold. He was a constant victim of deceit, betrayal, politics and politicians, both military and civilian. His intense feelings of grievance and injustice were not without justification, though his own defects of personality and character certainly contributed to his misfortunes.

Near the end of his career as an American general, he was placed in command of the Philadelphia area, the most unlikely place for him to be in the light of the constant rebuffs and rejection of influential, aristocratic groups despite his great ambition for success and acceptance by them. If there was a person who needed understanding and guidance, who needed a place where he would be respected and valued for his contribution to the American cause after his severe wounds at Saratoga, it was Arnold. Instead, he was given an impossible command in a hostile city and this contributed greatly to his defection. The Council of Pennsylvania was a band of single-minded, vindictive patriots who were bent on ruining General Arnold from the first. They were out to "get" him. Eventually this influential group demanded that the Congress court-martial him on a number of charges. At this time he was so disturbed and alienated that he wrote to Washington:

> If your Excellency thinks me criminal, for heaven's sake let me be immediately tried and, if found guilty, executed. I want no favour; I ask only justice. If this is denied me by your Excellency, I have nowhere to seek it but from the candid public, before whom I shall be under the necessity of laying the whole matter. Let me beg of you, Sir, to consider that a set of artful, unprincipled men in office may mis-

represent the most innocent actions and, by raising the public clamour against your Excellency, place you in the same situation I am in. Having made every sacrifice of fortune and blood, and become a cripple in the service of my country, I little expected to meet the ungrateful returns I have received from my countrymen; but as Congress have stamped ingratitude as a current coin, I must take it. I wish your Excellency, for your long and eminent service, may not be paid in the same coin. I have nothing left but the little reputation I have gained in the army. Delay in the present case is worse than death, and when it is considered that the President and council have had three months to produce the evidence, I cannot suppose the ordering a court-martial to determine the matter immediately, is the least precipitating it. I entreat that the court may be ordered to sit as soon as possible.[12]

At length, although he was acquitted of most of the charges against him, he received a reprimand. The reprimand was sufficiently galling and the public disgrace so painful that even the Council was somewhat regretful. But it was too late! Arnold, whose power strivings, aggressive demands, and uncultured ways, whose personal defects and social rejection interfered with his achieving unconditional acceptance, success, and triumph, became the first great American traitor and plummeted swiftly to execration. On the night of September 23, 1780, he defected to the British and was subsequently commissioned a brigadier general in the British army.

His name has become synonymous with treason, which has become an odious offense in all nations of the world. The denunciation of him by his countrymen remains without parallel. He was hanged or burned in effigy in Boston, Providence, Philadelphia, and scores of smaller places. In his own home state of Connecticut in New Milford, Middletown, and New Haven his effigy suffered particularly humiliating treatment, and in Norwich a mob stormed into the local cemetery and destroyed his father's tombstone because it bore the Arnold name. Washington said of him:

> From some traits of his character which have lately come to my knowledge, he seems to have been so hackneyed in villainy, and so lost to all sense of honor and shame that while his faculties will enable him to continue his sordid pursuits there will be no time for remorse.[13]

Arnold was never heroic or confident in exile. His defection to the British did not change his status; he was continually mistrusted and

[12] Willard M. Wallace, *Traitorous Hero* (New York: Harper & Brothers, 1954), p. 185. Reprinted with permission of the publisher.
[13] *Ibid.*, p. 270.

damned, and he never had a sense of recognition or belonging as a British general. One observer remarked:

> General Arnold is a very unpopular character in the British army, nor can all the patronage he meets with from the commander-in-chief procure him respectability. The subaltern officers have conceived such an aversion to him that they unanimously refused to serve under his command, and the detachment he is to lead was, on this account, officered from the Loyal American Corps.[14]

As a British officer, he was never given a real opportunity to attain significant victory. He was never given valorous recognition. He never achieved fame.

Unable to establish himself as an important commander, General Arnold went to live in England where he continued to search for a place of distinction and respectability. Every effort failed—both socially and financially. He never spoke of his traitorous behavior as an American general. It was to him a secret shame which he could not bring himself to face openly. When Tallyrand met him and asked him where he was traveling, he replied, "I am perhaps the only American who cannot give you letters for his own country—all the relations I had there are now broken—I must never return to the states." He refused to give his name, but Tallyrand recognized him and felt a deep sense of pity for him for he had witnessed his utter dejection and agony.

Certainly he was no longer the brilliant and courageous soldier. He was no longer even hopeful of any kind of success. He was totally alone in the world. He could never discuss his exploits as a general or any aspect of the life which had meant so much to him. He was no longer ambitious, no longer striving for fame. His life was a hopeless void. He was a ruined man, hated by the land of his nativity, despised, ignored, or forgotten in his new country, and ravaged by ill health and severe financial reverses. He died in poverty and debt. His tragic, lonely fate is horrible to conceive! How he struggled all his life to overcome the limits of his early environment, to attain respect, to become genuinely related to the reputable and cultured class. His powerful ambition and aggression grew out of a sense of isolation and estrangement from the desired in-group, even his act of treachery was a thrust for financial and social victory. In the end, his sense of alienation was complete. He was more violently cursed and anathematized, more totally cut-off than any other American soldier in our history. Yet he followed the only way he felt he could in reaction to political and social deceit, treachery, and rejection.

[14] *Ibid.*, p. 26.

Alger Hiss

No man in modern times has been more thoroughly castigated than Alger Hiss. A trusted government official who had a part in the creation of the United Nations Charter, he was indicted and found guilty of perjury with reference to espionage activities and communist affiliations. The prosecuting attorney, during his trials, called him another Benedict Arnold, another Judas Iscariot. Whether one believes Hiss was lying or not, perhaps the great need to punish him grew out of his unyielding refusal to acknowledge guilt. In America we make allowances for the penitent confessor, but we are particularly vengeful when the evidence points to a man's guilt and he absolutely refuses to concede any breach of conduct. The public mind may expiate the avowed evils of a man, even respect him for his public acknowledgment of guilt, but it does not ordinarily cherish innocence of thought, purity of values, and the ways of a good life. We are more sympathetic with confessions than we are rewarding of intransigent honesty. Perhaps this reflects the state of man's morals and ethics today. Modern man is not expected to say what he means, and he is not expected to do what he says particularly when he is seeking notoriety, status, and monetary gain. Sometimes we acclaim the reformed individual. Why is there such joy in America in defaming a man of good character and great reputation? Perhaps because we are all sinners at heart and fear our own public exposure.

Much of the hostile public clamor during the Hiss trials so clearly reflected in the newspapers and journals came about because Hiss would not confess. He maintained his story throughout. Perhaps his refusal to admit guilt was his real crime. We become annoyed with a man who is "evidently" lying but will not admit it. Perhaps we are threatened because he leaves a trace of doubt within us that our punishment is an act of grave injustice. We have to live with our conscience when we condemn a man who consistently maintains his innocence.

What happens to a man who has a reputable place in society, a responsible public position, which is dissipated, when social opinion turns against him? He becomes an estranged person, cut-off from his own talents and capacities, alienated from society, removed from the very sources of his own inner self. He is denied resources and opportunities for a creative life. He lives in isolation as a socially condemned and maligned person. Alger Hiss must have experienced terrible loneliness—maintaining his innocence throughout the terrible ordeal of committee investigations, Grand Jury hearings, and two public trials. He repeatedly claimed he was telling the truth, but he was not trusted or believed. In the end, he used all his resources, financial and otherwise, to prove that he had not been a Communist and that he had not stolen and photographed confidential government documents. He expended every energy to prove to his friends and the American people that he had not violated the trust placed in him. But finally, a jury decided he was lying. Alger Hiss claimed the hearings were unjust. He consistently maintained his innocence even though the antagonism against him increased; and, in the eyes of the public, he was worse than a thief because he would not confess his obvious crimes and would not beg to be forgiven. What terrible anguish he must have suffered—what bitter loneliness, what torments and tortures of the spirit, when increasingly and everywhere men who once trusted him turned away from him and doubted his integrity and veracity.

When Hiss first learned he had been accused of communist activities he immediately and publicly denied the charges. He requested a hearing before the Un-American Activities Committee to deny the charges under oath. From the beginning he felt the committee considered him guilty, with Mundt declaring "Certainly there is no hope for world peace under the leadership of men like Alger Hiss," even before his first hearing before the committee. He felt that some members of the committee had a political stake in punishing him and, more than the judge and jury, he felt he had been tried and found guilty by the committee. His associations with Whittaker Chambers were regularly and dramatically displayed by the committee, in hearings, reports, articles, speeches, and remarks to the press, radio, and television. He believed that Richard Nixon (who rose to fame as senator and vice-president after the Hiss trials and who came into the public eye as a result of them) was prejudiced against him from the first and was particularly bent on vilifying him. He discovered that Nixon had befriended Chambers. He quoted Chambers as follows:

> Senator Nixon's role did not end with his dash back to the United States to rally the House Committee when the microfilm was in its hands. His testimony before the Grand Jury that indicted Alger Hiss is a significant part of the Hiss Case. Throughout the most trying phases of the Case, Nixon and his family, and sometimes his parents, were at our farm, encouraging me and comforting my family. My children have caught him lovingly in a nickname. To them, he is always "Nixie," the kind and the good, about whom they will tolerate no nonsense. His somewhat martial Quakerism sometimes amused and always heartened me. I have a vivid picture of him, in the blackest hour of the Hiss Case, standing by the barn and saying in his quietly savage way (he is the

kindest of men): "If the American people understood the real character of Alger Hiss, they would boil him in oil." [15]

Specifically, Hiss was accused of perjury on two counts before the Grand Jury. These charges grew out of Chambers' story that he had seen Hiss every week or ten days from early 1935 until mid-April of 1938, and that from 1937 on he had come to Hiss' house regularly, at night, to receive from him State Department documents in their original form or in typewritten copies. Hiss' denial of these charges led the Grand Jury to indict him for perjury. Yet this same Grand Jury failed to indict Chambers who admitted he had perjured himself.

Hiss felt the loneliness of not being listened to, not being understood, not being trusted. In the second trial (the first ended in the jury's failure to render a verdict) Hiss felt he could no longer call on former friends—the public bias and hostility had become so great.

> It seemed as though strong forces would attack any step, however justified, that was taken in my behalf—jurors, judge, witnesses all were vilified. As with the attacks on Judge Kaufman (the presiding judge in the first trial) and the jurors the effect on these attacks was definite. Because we did not wish to cause further attacks on the two justices (of the Supreme Court) who had known me well enough to be qualified to testify as to my character, we did not ask them to testify at the next trial.[16]

Alger Hiss felt he had not had a just and unbiased trial. He felt he was tried by slanted articles in newspapers and radio reports in which a verdict of guilty with the maximum penalty was urged. He felt he was condemned by members of the Un-American Activities Committee who continuously persecuted him in the hearings and pronounced him guilty in public statements. The trials against avowed Communists were held in the same courtroom during Hiss' first trial. Judith Coplin (a government worker caught with confidential documents in her possession) was being judged during the second trial. Both these hearings fanned public resentment against Hiss.

Whether one believes Hiss was too dishonest or too honest, whether one believes he was crafty or naïve, whether one believes he was crucified by political ambitions and a hostile anticommunist feeling sweeping America at the time, or whether one believes his punishment and imprisonment were justified, the tragedy remains that he has maintained

---

[15] Alger Hiss, *In the Court of Public Opinion* (New York: Alfred A. Knopf, Inc., 1957), p. 191. Reprinted by permission of the publisher.
[16] *Ibid.*, pp. 295-296.

his innocence and continues to search for evidence which will ferret out the truth. The tragedy remains that he has been deprived of a creative public life and society has been deprived of his valuable talents and resources. Mr. Hiss continues to suffer defamation of character and the social rejection of an unreconstructed rebel. His rebellion is his refusal to accept the verdict of the American people that he is guilty of perjury and espionage. This struggle, this determination to be vindicated in the court of public opinion, means he must continue to use his resources to defend. Being cut-off and alienated from his society, his only solution is that of a lonely person whose achievement or glory remains in the past.

Perhaps the entire truth may some day be revealed, a truth which both Chambers and Hiss could honor, one which would enable Hiss to live as a creative person, using his creative mind and capabilities to enhance himself and human life everywhere in the world. Only the future can determine what the torment and utter loneliness and dejection Hiss has experienced in being publicly damned will lead him to do but it already seems clear that he has achieved a depth of sensitivity and awareness, that he has come to himself as a person in a way that only lonely suffering could have helped him achieve. He may have lost his place in society but he has gained his own self. He has come to himslf through hardship, and suffering, and through a sense of separation, social isolation, and private internment. He has been forced to examine his life and to depend for his nourishment and growth on his own being. In doing so, he has exercised self-potentialities, realized a depth of human experience, and known an affinity to nature and life which are beyond the insights and awarenesses of ordinary men. In the fullest sense, he has come to be a courageous man in the hours of deepest pain when he had to stand entirely alone

Whittaker Chambers

In exposing Alger Hiss, Whittaker Chambers believed he was opening before the world, in a compelling way, the inevitable clashing of two irreconcilable forces in modern life, Communism and Freedom. Mr. Chambers identified himself with Freedom and associated Hiss with Communism. Yet this issue which motivated Chambers to denounce Communists in America was never recognized as significant by millions of Americans who were concerned primarily with the question of who was telling the truth. The general public failed to understand his mission and Mr. Chambers keenly felt the vitriolic contempt of people in numerous and widespread attacks against him. In his own words, he conveys the feeling of being victimized, exclaiming:

> Against me was an almost solid line-up of the most powerful groups of men in the country, the bitterly hostile reaction of much of the press, the smiling skepticism of much of the public, the venomous calumnies of the Hiss forces, the all but universal failure to understand the real meaning of the Case or my real purpose.[17]

The almost violent opposition, the sudden aloofness of former friends and the outright withdrawal of others, made Chambers realize how utterly alone he was in the world. He began to sense the weight of his own personal inadequacies and the enormous futility of his efforts. He longed for solitude, for isolation. He could not bear the torment of constant condemnation. He wished to be completely alone. As the pain increased, slowly, gradually, then suddenly, he wished not to be at all. For him, as the hearings proceeded, a physical freezing settled around his heart, a feeling of such total repulsion that he died in spirit and will long before the wish for physical death overcame him.

Loneliness for Whittaker Chambers did not begin with the Hiss-Chambers confrontation. From his earliest years, he suffered a deep sense of alienation from his family, from other children, and from his teachers. His had been an extremely difficult birth, a painful, torturous ordeal of which his mother never ceased to remind him. She gave him the name Jay Vivian which he deeply hated, and which he changed as soon as he was able. The initial experience of being singled out for rebuke and ridicule by other children occurred on his first day of school. His name was called by his teacher and a loud ripple of laughter swept the other children and resounded in his ears long after the incident was over. It left him feeling bitter and loathsome. He soon hated school and everything about it. His torment continued throughout public school and left deep emotional scars to remind him of his odious nature. His family could give him no support against the alien world, for within his life in the family there was a marked, weird separation, an absence of genuine love and respect, and beyond this a cold familial atmosphere and an indefinable, pervasive sense of doom. He was constantly at odds with his mother and father and in very different ways. He was frequently belittled and made to feel worthless. He was often subjected to a bizarre, extremely inhuman, and unhealthy family existence. To escape the

[17] Whittaker Chambers, *Witness* (New York: Random House, Inc., 1952), pp. 20-21. Copyright © 1952 by Whittaker Chambers; reprinted by permission of the publisher.

malady of life in school and the malady of life at home, Mr. Chambers sought refuge in the fields and woods. Here he could live quietly, in silence. Here he would not be harassed by the jests and raillery of his classmates or broken in self-esteem and confidence by his family. In nature he could find temporary peace and some joy. He could see and hear and feel at one with growing life. Even at night the loneliness of the woods was never as disturbing as the presence of people by daylight. The woods were his haven in a world filled with pain and rejection.

Loneliness pervaded his early life wherever he went. The loneliness at home and school increasingly destroying his sense of value and his feeling for humanity while the loneliness in the woods gave him strength to live and enabled him to relate to nature at a time when no other relationship was possible.

As he reached young manhood, the tragic suicidal death of his brother nearly destroyed him. This death severely increased his bitterness and sense of resentment against the deteriorating values of society. He cursed the world as vulgar, stupid, complacent, inhumane, materialistic. He felt that the toxins of a slowly decaying world poisoned all life within it, that the human world had died in soul and in essential values, that there was nothing in life to facilitate genuine growth and healthy relatedness. He had struggled a long, long time to keep his brother alive, saving him repeatedly only at the last moment from successful suicide. This death was not only a terribly lonely lamentation and mourning but it was like a final blow, a crushing psychic defeat to Whittaker who had so little to love. His feeling of terrible loneliness and desolation is conveyed in a poem he wrote as he left his brother's burial place for the last time.

> Fall on me, snow,
> Cover me up;
> Cover the houses and the streets.
> Let me see only in the light of another year
> The roofs and the minds that killed him,
> And the earth that holds him,
> Forever dead.[18]

At last, he felt he found the answer. The only hope for the world would come through communism. He believed this for some years and worked for the communist goals until his direct experience enabled him to realize that communism violated fundamental religious truths and

---

[18] *Ibid.*, p. 187. Copyright © 1952 by Whittaker Chambers; reprinted by permission of Random House, Inc.

threatened freedom of life everywhere in the world. His thinking changed radically as he sought to expose the destructive components of communism and to reveal to the world how communism violates the soul, and God, and freedom. He was willing to disturb the tranquil life he knew on a farm with his wife and two children and his position as a senior editor with *Time* magazine because he believed that disclosing the names of the Communists he had associated with, many of whom had been in the State Department, would be a resounding victory for God and freedom in America. With each informing came the certain conviction that something within him was dying. What was dying was his right to live, his right to be a person, his right to work and develop his potentialities. He realized he could not destroy another human being without at the same time degrading and destroying himself. Mr. Chambers describes in the following passages the meaning and impact of being a witness against men he had respected and even loved.

> There is in men a very deep-rooted instinct that they may not inform against those whose kindness and affection thay have shared, at whose tables they have eaten and under whose roofs they have slept, whose wives and children they have known as friends—and that regardless of who those others are or what crimes they have committed. It is an absolute prohibition. It is written in no book, but it is more binding than any code that exists. If of necessity a man must violate that prohibition, and it is part of the tragedy of history that, for the greater good, men sometimes must, the man who violates it must do so in the full consciousness that there is a penalty. That penalty is a kind of death, most deadly if a man must go on living. It is not violent. It is not even a deepening shadow. It is a simple loss of something as when a filter removes all color from the light.[19]

He could not free his mind from the organic revulsion he experienced with every word of denunciation, with every accusation. His sense of tragic doom, the spirit of loneliness so compelling in his childhood and youth came to the fore, again disrupting the peaceful years of marriage and fatherhood and his productive work with *Time* magazine. The pressures were personal, social, editorial, disruptive, slanderous, and, above all, unremitting. He was constantly subjected to insubordination, hostility, and insulting behavior by members of his own staff.

In the end, he felt he must testify against the Communists he had known. He felt he could not be spared, that this, however revolting, was the whole purpose of his existence—to awaken America against the evils of communism, to alert America to the dangers and secretive activities

[19] *Ibid.*, p. 720.

that are being plotted in tunnels and in the dark and behind closed doors. Testifying meant he would be execrated, and, though he would vilify others, not doing so meant he would deny his only mission in life and destroy his own soul. So he chose to tell his story—all of it—but as he did the meaning and value of work and life and love died too.

His powerful friends, who might have been expected to help him, were distinguished chiefly by a prudent use of their resources. Whittaker Chambers was more alone than he ever thought possible during hearings before the Un-American Activities Committee, the New York Grand Jury, and the two public trials, the last of which ended in the conviction of Alger Hiss.

> I was master neither of the situation nor of anything else. My sole thought was to endure a situation that I felt in prospect, and much more acutely while it was going on, as pure horror. In face of that intensely hostile crowd and the ordeal of taking the stand publicly again, I scarcely cared whether or not the hearing was all that stood between me and powerful enemies.[20]

The pain was sometimes overwhelming. The constant glares and attacks were exhausting. He often experienced the strongest feeling of being treated with blistering condescension of being looked upon as a kind of human filth. He was aware of hidden meanings and unrelentless nuances of expression playing over him directed towards breaking him. It brought an eerie, creepy feeling which aroused suspicion in him and kept him filled with tension, shook him, and affected his ability to speak and think sharply and clearly. He would slip to his knees, bowed down with worry and fear, and pray to find peace within his heart and soul, pray for the strength to continue.

From the beginning, he felt that the press had sought to break him. It was an attitude very hard to bear because it was set like cement. There was no way to counteract it. There was no defense against it. He felt the whole world beyond the borders of his farm surging out against him, motivated by curiosity, hostility, or simple intellectual prejudice. No depravity was too bizarre to "explain his motives." No speculation was too fantastic, no interpretation too preposterous to uncover the "disturbed, psychopathic" nature of his personality. All kinds of doctrines were discovered to account for his "distorted visions." He felt deeply alone too when he saw that the nation considered the battle between Hiss and himself a grudge fight, when he saw that the nation would not accept as fact that his only purpose was to defeat the forces of commu-

---

[20] *Ibid.,* p. 628.

nism in America and to glorify freedom of thought and a Christian way of life. He could not make others see that it was a life and death struggle for democracy, not simply a matter of who lied and who told the truth. Unable to communicate his vital message, he felt increasingly alienated, increasingly lonely. He wondered that no friend ever came, ever penetrated to the roots of his function and responsibility as a witness. No person ever genuinely understood his call. In the whole nation there was no priest, no minister, no fellow Quaker, no neighbor who truly grasped what he was trying to do. No one ever came to him to say, "I do not want to ask or to tell you anything. I simply want you to know I am with you." There was no one at all. No one ever came.

He felt he had already caused his family irrevocable loss and grief. He could not share with them the vast torment of his testimony and examination. He laid himself open to God, sought guidance in prayer, let himself enter into the spiritual silences of the universe. Emptied of thought and feeling, he was momentarily delivered of his wretchedness and his terrible isolation, and in its place was an image, the image of a Russian revolutionist who, as the only protest he was able to make against the flogging of his fellow prisoners, drenched himself in kerosene, ignited himself and burned himself to death. Desperately, more and more he wished to be by himself, alone. At one point the pain of loneliness, the suffering in being mistreated, misunderstood, and mistrusted, and the restrictiveness of not being able to share his experience with any one were so great that he attempted suicide.

Everything in his life, his every act seemed futile. All the torment, suffering, attack and counterattack, were entirely futile, contributing to his sense of total defeat and his sense that he had misunderstood life with consequent disaster to all he met. He was reaching the limit of his strength to go on. He felt that no act less extreme than his abortive suicide could have disciplined him to be able to endure the public tirade and rebuke which he was to face until the trials came to an end. From the experience, he took away the indispensable certainty that all he ever had a right to pray to God for was the strength equal to meet necessity.

Whether Whittaker Chambers told the truth or perpetrated a grand impersonation of unmatched deception, he lost his sense of value in life and his existence became a static one. His vast reservoir of literary talent, his keen mind, his rare ability to depict in a deep significant way issues of human consequence now remain unexpressed in a veritable wasteland. Alger Hiss has deeply suffered too—a brilliant career has been cut short—a talented American has been deeply wounded. Was

Chambers' mission successful? Has communism suffered a severe defeat in America? Have freedom, peace, individuality, creativity, been advanced? Has anything constructive happened as the result of the Hiss Case? Mr. Chambers answers these questions himself. He believes the world has become even more threatening, and cold, and lonely. He believes the world is heading for an even more terrible witness or total disaster. His last years, as he describes them in *Witness*, are tragic.

For myself, I now view the stars with the curiosity of any man who wonders in what form his soul may soon be venturing among them. For the Hiss Case has turned my wife and me into old people—not a disagreeable condition. But we who used to plan in terms of decades, now find a year, two years, the utmost span of time we can take in. Repeatedly, in this last autumn of unseasonable warmth, my wife has drawn me out to stand with her among our gardens, once so pleasant, now overgrown with weeds, because, as we say, neither of us really fooling the other, we no longer can find time to tend them. It is not time that we cannot find. Repeatedly, my wife has planned what we must do to bring them back to life. We do not do it. I do not think we shall unless time itself can lift from us the sense that we have lived our lives and the rest is a malingering.

This, which we both feel, we force ourselves seldom to entertain as a thought. For, with us, discipline must take the place of energy in that life to which it is our children, of course, who bind us. It is for them that we run through the routines of our days, outwardly cheerful, for we count among our blessings the fact that, a very few years more, and we shall be safely dispensable. Our trouble is that the smallest things now have power to disturb our precarious self-discipline—an unkindness, a meanness, or, on a greater scale, a sudden insight into the smugness of the world before its vast peril, or an occasional reminder that we are still beset by enemies that are powerful and vindictive. Then it becomes an effort to sustain those formal good spirits that are our hourly improvisation—the necessary grace notes to lead the ear away from the groundbass which is our reality. For there are kinds of music that the world should not hear.

In the countryside, people are already beginning to plan for the spring which they can sense, like a thaw-wind, just beyond the drift of winter. It is three years since I have been able to plough a field on this farm. I have sometimes thought that, if, in this coming spring, my son and I could simply work and seed a field and watch it sprout, an absolute healing would follow. Or my wife and I have sometimes said that a year, or even six months, completely unharried by the world and its agencies, would refit us for struggle. For it is a season of peace that, like the world, we most crave, and, like the world, are most unlikely to get. Failing that, our spirits fall back upon an ultimate petition where our fears and hopes are one. . . . In a world grown older and colder, my wife and I have no dearer wish for ourselves—when our time shall have come, when our children shall be grown, when the witness that was laid on us shall have lost its meaning because our whole world will have borne a more terrible witness or it will no longer exist.[21]

It is sad to read these words, to see Whittaker Chambers dying, immobilized, paralyzed, unable, insensitive to the riches of life. It is heartrending to feel his stationary existence as he waits to die, to know his talents and potentialities lay buried in a passive, meaningless life. What a terrible loss! Here is a man with vast potentialities, a rare skill of perceptiveness and sensitivity and insight. Here is a man with a precious ability to see through to the heart of events and issues and to articulate them broadly, genuinely, uniquely, in a beautiful, elegant, creative literary style. Here is a man who thinks for himself, who experiences deeply enough and writes artistically enough to require his audience to contemplate and relate—not simply to read but to give serious consideration and meditation to important questions, issues, and values of our time. Here is a gifted man who speaks no more.

[21] *Ibid.*, pp. 798-799.

VI

THE VALUE OF LONELINESS

To love is to be lonely. Every love eventually is broken by illness, separation, or death. The exquisite nature of love, the unique quality or dimension in its highest peak, is threatened by change and termination, and by the fact that the loved one does not always feel or know or understand. In the absence of the loved one, in solitude and loneliness, a new self emerges, in solitary thought. The loneliness quickens love and brings to it new perceptions and sensitivities, and new experiences of mutual depth and beauty.

All love leads to suffering. If we did not care for others in a deep and fundamental way, we would not experience grief when they are troubled or disturbed, when they face tragedy or misfortune, when they are ill and dying. Every person is ultimately confronted with the pain of separation or death, with tragic grief which can be healed in silence and isolation. When pain is accepted and felt as one's own, at the center of being, then suffering grows into compassion for other human beings and all living creatures. Through pain, the heart opens and out of the sorrow come new sensations of levity and joy.

All suffering which is accepted and received with dignity eventuates in deepened sensitivity. One cannot be sensitive without knowing loneliness. To see is to be lonely—to hear, feel, touch—every vital, solitary experience of the senses is a lonely one. Anyone who senses with a wide range of delicate feelings and meanings experiences loneliness. To be open to life in an authentic sense is to be lonely, for in such openness one hears and feels and senses beyond the ordinary. Through loneliness we are refined and sensitized and open to life's lofty ideals and influences. We are enabled to grow in awareness, in understanding, in aesthetic capabilities, in human relations.

Loneliness has a quality of immediacy and depth, it is a significant experience—one of the few in modern life—in which man communes with himself. And in such communion man comes to grips with his own being. He discovers life, who he is, what he really wants, the meaning of his existence, the true nature of his relations with others. He sees and realizes for the first time truths which have been obscured for a long time. His distortions suddenly become naked and transparent. He perceives himself and others with a clearer, more valid vision and understanding.

In absolutely solitary moments man experiences truth, beauty, nature, reverence, humanity. Loneliness enables one to return to a life with others with renewed hope and vitality, with a fuller dedication, with a deeper desire to come to a healthy resolution of problems and issues involving others, with possibility and hope for a rich, true life with others.

Loneliness keeps open the doors to an expanding life. In utter loneliness, one can find answers to living, one can find new values to live by, one can see a new path or direction. Something totally new is revealed.

In the dark, despairing hours, sometimes only through loneliness can the individual bear to return to confront ugly faces and listen to criticism, and experience hurts inflicted by those one loves most. When one has felt totally forlorn, desolate, and abandoned, one can arrive at a new depth of companionship and a new sense of joy and belonging. When man can leave himself to his own loneliness, he can return to himself with a new commitment to his fellow man. Not an escape from loneliness, or a plan, not strategy and resolution, but direct facing of one's loneliness with courage, letting be all that is in its fullness, this is a requirement of creative living. To be worthy of one's loneliness is an ultimate challenge, a challenge which if realized, strengthens the person and puts him more fully in touch with his own resources. At first, the experience of loneliness may be frightening, even terrifying, but as one submits to the pain and suffering and solitude, one actually reaches himself, listens to the inner voice and experiences a strange new confidence. The individual is restored to himself and life again becomes meaningful and worthwhile.

The lonely sufferer helps himself to a fuller realization of self, not by reducing his sense of pain and isolation, but by bringing its full extent and magnitude to consciousness. Great loneliness and suffering are met creatively, as potential growth experiences, only by surrendering to them, fully and completely. Salvation, self-growth, lies in giving full assent to loneliness and suffering, accepting what is, not fighting or resisting, not rationalizing or appealing to external helps, not demanding to know why one has been singled out for so much pain, but submitting one's self to the experience in total self-surrender. Whoever is able to bear loneliness grows to the stature of his experience. Loneliness paves the way to healing, to true compassion, to intimate bonds with all living creatures and all aspects of nature and the universe.

The "never be lonely" theme is a reflection of man's estrangement from himself in the world today. When an individual avoids facing directly a situation which contains the seeds of loneliness, he alienates himself from his own capacity for being lonely and from the possibility for fundamental social ties and empathy. It is not loneliness which separates the person from others but the terror of loneliness and the constant effort to escape it. We must learn to care for our own loneliness and suffering and the loneliness and suffering of others, for within pain and isolation and loneliness one can find courage and hope and what is brave and lovely and true in life. Serving loneliness is a way to self-identity and to love, and faith in the wonder of living.

The moments between death and creation, the periods between the end and the beginning, the interval between completion and starting of a significant project are often times of deep loneliness. But in these intervals the individual can come to self-truths, to new strengths, and to new directions. Loneliness is often a painful and restless time. It leaves its traces in man but these are marks of pathos, of weathering, which enhance dignity and maturity and beauty, and which open new possibilities for tenderness and love.

Loneliness is as much a reality of life as night and rain and thunder, and it can be lived creatively, as any other experience. So I say, let there be loneliness, for where there is loneliness there is also sensitivity, and where there is sensitivity, there is awareness and recognition and promise.

Being lonely and being related are dimensions of an organic whole, both necessary to the growth of individuality and to the deepening value and enrichment of friendship. Let there be loneliness, for where there is loneliness, there also is love, and where there is suffering, there also is joy.

BIBLIOGRAPHY

Alvarez, Walter C., "Your Health," *The Detroit News* (June 19, 1959).

Angle, Paul M., *The Lincoln Reader*. New Brunswick, N. J.: Rutgers University Press, 1947.

Bartek, Johnny, *Life Out There*. New York: Charles Scribner's Sons, 1943.

Bowers, Claude G., "The Statesman" in *The Greatness of Woodrow Wilson*, ed. Em Bowles Alsop. New York: Holt, Rinehart and Winston, 1956.

Bowman, Claude C., "Loneliness and Social Change," *American Journal of Psychiatry*, 112 (1955), 194-198.

Breckinridge, Elizabeth, *Community Services for Older People*. Chicago: Wilcox and Follett Co., 1952.

Brown, Rollo Walter, *Lonely Americans*. New York: Coward-McCann, Inc., 1929.

Buhl, Hermann, *Lonely Challenge*, trans., Hugh Merrick. New York: E. P. Dutton & Co., Inc., 1956.

Burgess, Perry, *Who Walk Alone*. New York: Holt, Rinehart and Winston, 1940.

Byrd, Richard E., *Alone*. New York: G. P. Putnam's Sons, 1938.

Chambers, Whittaker, *Witness*. New York: Random House, Inc., 1952.

Chase, Richard, *Emily Dickinson*. New York: William Sloane Associates, 1951.

Chesterton, G. K., *Come To Think Of It*. New York: Dodd, Mead & Co., 1931.

Cooke, Alistair, *Generation on Trial: U.S.A. v. Alger Hiss*. New York: Alfred A. Knopf, Inc., 1950.

Dabney, Virginius, "The Human Being" in *The Greatness of Woodrow Wilson*, ed. Em Bowles Alsop. New York: Holt, Rinehart and Winston, 1956.

Day, Donald, ed., *Woodrow Wilson's Own Story*. Boston: Little, Brown & Company, 1952.

de Toledano, Ralph and Victor Lasky, *Seeds of Treason*. New York: Funk & Wagnalls, 1950.

Detroit Free Press, "Brought Together in Loneliness, Oldsters Part in Bitterness" (August 18, 1959).

Dickinson, Emily, *The Complete Poems of Emily Dickinson*. Boston: Little, Brown & Company, 1927.

Flexner, James T., *The Traitor and the Spy*. New York: Harcourt, Brace & World, Inc., 1953.

Form of Prayers for the Day of Atonement, rev. ed. (English translation), New York: Hebrew Publishing Co.

Fromm, Erich, *Escape From Freedom*. New York: Holt, Rinehart and Winston, Inc., 1941.

Fromm-Reichmann, Frieda, "Loneliness," *Psychiatry*, 22 (1959), 1-16.

Gibran, Kahlil, *The Madman*. New York: Alfred A. Knopf Co., 1918.

Herndon, William and Jesse W. Weik, *Abraham Lincoln*, Vols. I and II. New York: Appleton-Century-Crofts, Inc., 1920.

Hill, Ruth, "Old Age At the Crossroads" in *New Goals for Old Age*, ed. George Lawton. New York: Columbia University Press, 1943.

Hiss, Alger, *In The Court of Public Opinion*. New York: Alfred A. Knopf, Inc., 1957.

Holmes, Oliver Wendell, "The Profession of Law" in *Speeches*. Boston: Little, Brown & Company, 1913.

Hutt, Max L. and Robert G. Gibby, *Child: Development and Adjustment*. Englewood Cliffs, N. J.: Allyn & Bacon, 1959.

Johnson, Thomas H., *Emily Dickinson*. Cambridge, Mass.: Harvard University Press, 1955.

Johnson, Thomas H., ed., *The Poems of Emily Dickinson*, Vols. I, II, and III. Cambridge, Mass.: The Belknap Press of Harvard University Press, 1955.

Johnson, Thomas H. and Theodora V. W. Ward, eds., *The Letters of Emily Dickinson*, Vols. I, II, and III. Cambridge, Mass.: The Belknap Press of Harvard University Press, 1958.

London and Foreign Bible Society. *The Holy Bible*. London: Eyre and Spottiswoods, Ltd.

Mabie, Hamilton W., *Fruits of the Spirit*. New York: Dodd, Mead & Co., 1917.

May, Rollo, Ernest Angel, and Henri F. Ellenberger, *Existence—A New Dimension in Psychiatry and Psychology*. New York: Basic Books, Inc., 1958.

McGill, Ralph, "The President" in *The Greatness of Woodrow Wilson*, ed. Em Bowles Alsop. New York: Holt, Rinehart and Winston, 1956.

Menninger, Karl, *Love Against Hate*. New York: Harcourt, Brace & World, Inc., 1942.

Miles, L. Wardlaw, *The Tender Realist and Other Essays*. New York: Holt, Rinehart and Winston, 1930.

Moustakas, Clark E., "Creativity, Conformity, and the Self" in *Creativity and Psychological Health*, ed. Michael Andrews. Syracuse: Syracuse University Press, (in press).

Overstreet, Bonaro W., *Understanding Fear in Ourselves and Others*. New York: Harper & Brothers, 1951.

Rice, A. H., *Happiness Road*. New York: Appleton-Century-Crofts, Inc., 1942.

Riesman, David, Reuel Denney, and Nathan Glazer, *The Lonely Crowd*. New Haven, Conn.: Yale University Press, 1950.

Robertson, James, *Young Children In Hospitals*. New York: Basic Books, Inc., 1959.

Rogers, Carl R. and Rosalind F. Dymond, eds., *Psychotherapy and Personality Change*. Chicago: University of Chicago Press, 1954.

Saint-Exupéry, Antoine de, *The Little Prince*, trans. Katherine Woods. New York: Harcourt, Brace & World, Inc., 1943.

———, *Night Flight*, trans. Stuart Gilbert. New York: Appleton-Century-Crofts, Inc., 1937.

————, *Wind, Sand, and Stars*, trans. Lewis Galantiere. New York: Reynal & Hitchcock, 1939.

————, *Wisdom of the Sands*, trans. Stuart Gilbert. Harcourt, Brace & World, Inc., 1950.

Sandburg, Carl, *Abraham Lincoln: The Prairie Years and The War Years*. New York: Harcourt, Brace & World, Inc., 1954.

Scruggs, Anderson, *Ritual For Myself*. New York: The MacMillan Company, 1941.

Steiner, Lee R., *Where Do People Take Their Troubles?* Boston: Houghton Mifflin Company, 1945.

Sullivan, Harry Stack, *The Interpersonal Theory of Psychiatry*. New York: W. W. Norton & Co., 1953.

Tabor, Eithne, *The Cliff's Edge: Songs of a Psychotic*. New York: Sheed & Ward Inc., 1950.

Thoreau, Henry David, *Walden and Other Writings*, ed. Brooks Atkinson (Modern Library). New York: Random House, Inc., 1937.

Truman, Harry S., *Memoirs: Years of Decisions*, Vol. I. New York: Doubleday & Co., 1955.

————, *Memoirs: Years of Trial and Hope*, Vol. II. New York: Doubleday & Co., 1956.

United States Court of Appeals. *United States of America Against Alger Hiss*. Transcript of Record and Documents. Vols. I-X.

Wallace, Willard M., *Traitorous Hero*. New York: Harper & Brothers, 1954.

Whittaker, James C., *We Thought We Heard The Angels Sing*. New York: E. P. Dutton & Co., Inc., 1943.

Whyte, William H., Jr., *The Organization Man*. New York: Simon and Schuster, Inc., 1956.

Wolfe, Thomas, *The Hills Beyond*. New York: Harper & Brothers, 1941.

Wood, Margaret, *Paths of Loneliness*. New York: Columbia University Press, 1953.

TWENTIETH CENTURY VIEWS

American Authors

TWENTIETH CENTURY VIEWS

British Authors